*Pacesetters*

# The Border Runners

**James Irungu and
James Shimanyula**

MACMILLAN

First published 1984
Reprinted 1984, 1986, 1987, 1988, 1991, 1992

Published by THE MACMILLAN PRESS LTD
London and Basingstoke
*Associated companies and representatives in Accra,
Auckland, Delhi, Dublin, Gaborone, Hamburg, Harare,
Hong Kong, Kuala Lumpur, Lagos, Manzini, Melbourne,
Mexico City, Nairobi, New York, Singapore, Tokyo.*

ISBN 0−333−35412−5

Printed in Hong Kong

# Macmillan *Pacesetters*

# Chapter 1

'Let us muse over the nightmare ahead of us,' Muna suggested. He was seventeen years of age, a well-groomed, dark young man whose face suggested he was of a serious turn of mind. He was in a comfortably furnished dining room, with plastered mud walls. He was standing and had spoken to a young man who was having a nap on a couch and a teenage girl who was tidying up the room absent-mindedly. If the man had heard the boy, he did not reveal it but continued to rest with an open novel on his face. But the girl was upset. She paused in the act of sweeping the floor and looked up at Muna piteously.

'I'd rather not think about it,' she said. 'It would drive me mad.'

'No one likes to think about unpleasant things,' said Muna, 'but the hardships of life are a reality which cannot be ignored. No matter how hard you try to keep it out of your mind, it keeps on coming back to you, doesn't it?'

'Yes,' she agreed, 'and I cannot believe it has happened to us. How did we get into the mess anyhow?'

She went to the man lying on the couch and stood looking down at him, her face bitter. 'You know, don't you, Waichari? Tell us how.'

'Peace,' the man mumbled.

1

'We have a right to know, since we are going to suffer for it. I have noticed you've had some secret worry this year. But you never told us. Now we know what it was. But how did it happen? What did you want such a large amount of money for? Has the burden been too big for you?'

'Peace,' the man mumbled again.

'Let us discuss it as a family,' she went on. 'We are not children any longer and you have been aloof long enough.'

'Leave the worrying to me,' the man mumbled without moving as he lay on the couch. 'Leave me alone.'

'How can we help worrying with such a threat hanging over us?' Tears were beginning to glint in her eyes. 'You have failed, Waichari. Within a year. Wake up and admit it! Tell us where we are heading. Where? Where?'

The simple, L-shaped house in which they were talking was on top of a hill on a twelve-acre farm. Below this old-fashioned house was a larger and more modern one under construction. Below the home compound was a paddock with a few cattle, and beyond this were a few thousand coffee trees. In the valley was the vegetable garden. The farm was typical of those which filled the hilly, green district. Towards the west stretched the range of mountains called Nyandarua.

Here, the little family had been brought up. Their father, Mathu, was a diligent person who never looked back. Unschooled, he had gone to the city as a boy to look for work. There he eventually made enough money to raise a dowry for a wife. His sister chose for him an industrious girl called Martha and she bore him a son, Waichari, and much later another son, Muna, and a daughter, Waitherero.

Shortly after land consolidation a few years before Independence, Mathu returned to the countryside with his savings and gave his wife the enormous task of clearing the land he had inherited from his fathers, planting cash crops and rearing cattle, while he himself hired a shop in the local trading centre. This was a wise move, for after the first five difficult years of settling down, the family made gradual progress.

With his business firmly established and the farm yielding well, Mathu was able to turn his attention during the next five years to building up a plot of land and a wholesale store. Delighted by his success, he became more ambitious. The improvement of rural development as well as rising coffee prices fanned his ambition.

His next project over the following five years was to save for a lorry and a family car. It was successful also, for at the end of that period he had landed a new nine-ton lorry and an old station wagon.

Mathu had more cause to rejoice than over mere material possessions. His children were growing up to his expectations. Waichari, the first born, proved to be as business-minded as his father and he was expected to run the store after his father's retirement. Mathu's only anxiety was that, though Waichari was cool and quietly spoken, he had a wild streak in him, but Mathu hoped his son would settle down in time.

Muna, the second born, was brilliant. Mathu had no doubt he would make it to higher school and then to the university, to be the pride of the family.

Waitherero was as invaluable to her mother at home and on the farm as Waichari was to his father at the store. She was not lacking in sense either, and was a dutiful, adorable daughter.

Generally, Mathu considered his children to be a blessing. His main concern was to go on expanding until he was a big shot. After purchasing the vehicles, he embarked on his next five-year project. He had noticed that, with the boosting of prices, the people of this tea and coffee growing region were demolishing the old mud houses and erecting stone ones. Not to be left behind, Mathu started building a five-bedroom house below the old one.

Unfortunately, one morning, as Mathu and his wife were speeding down a treacherous hill in their station wagon, Mathu miscalculated in steering round a bend and the vehicle took off into the air like an aeroplane. It came back to earth with the force of a crashing meteor; the twisted wreck burst into flames and after a while it exploded. It was a terrible death for the industrious couple.

The death of their parents the year before had hit the children hard. Muna and Waitherero had noticed that Waichari's spirits, instead of improving with the passage of time, were getting worse, especially during the past few months. They had known then that something else was worrying him, but he never confided in them. Now they knew what it was. They had seen one of the notices which had been stuck to walls in the trading centre that day. It said that certain lawyers, acting on behalf of their client, a certain bank, were going to have their own farm as well as their plot sold within two weeks by public auction, unless a sum of eleven thousand pounds and all costs were paid to them before then. Waith-erero could not believe that it had happened to them, and was asking Waichari how it had happened and where they were heading.

'Wherever the wind may blow us,' he answered her, still lying immobile with his face covered by the novel. 'Now, will you please leave me alone?'

The tears which had been forming in Waitherero's eyes spilled over and two drops trickled down her thin cheeks. 'Poverty looms ahead and all you can tell me is to leave you alone!' She turned away from him, wiping her tears, and sank on to a sofa where she sat sniffing.

Moving in slow motion, Waichari removed the novel from his face, swung his legs on to the floor and sat up. He was a tall, slim man in his late twenties, casually dressed. He had lean, dark brown features like Waitherero's, but his were marred by a permanently hard expression. Unkempt hair and a moustache did not help to improve it. It was difficult to guess his feelings as he studied his weeping sister steadily with narrowed eyes.

'The trouble with you, little sister,' he told her in his lazy, low voice, 'is that you are too emotional. This is a matter I can sort out. Set your mind at ease and have faith in me.'

'Have faith in you!' she sobbed. 'How can I have faith after you have led us into such a pit after only a year. Poor, precious Daddy, if he were alive we wouldn't be in such a fix.'

Waichari started to retort sarcastically and then he stopped. He had been about to tell her that it was her precious Daddy who had dug that pit for them. But how could he speak ill of his own father – such a father – and how would it help? How could he disillusion her, since she had such a lovely memory of him? Besides, how could the old man have known he was going to die and leave his children in such a mess? No, the old man should be left to lie in peace with his character untarnished. Let Waitherero and the world at large blame him, Waichari, for the mess, no matter how unpleasant it was for him.

On the face of it, Waichari had inherited material wealth, but after the funeral he had gone to see the old man's bank manager to find out about his financial position, and what he found out shocked him. The old man had borrowed a quarter of a million shillings which were supposed to be repaid over a period of three years, with due interest. The bank had for security the title deeds of the farm as well as the plot. After that, Waichari had had more bad news. The motor company from which the lorry had been bought claimed a balance of thirty thousand shillings. There was also a small amount due to the architect. Waichari wondered how on earth his father had expected to meet these obligations. The old man had been no fool, and must have had plans for making the extra income.

Waichari made rough estimates for the first year. Fortunately, business and farming were excellent for most of the country that year and Waichari estimated he could raise five thousand pounds in profit. Yet even if he raised more than he had estimated, since the year was the best ever, it was inevitable that he would find himself short of cash. He had really tried. He had paid off the architect but suspended the construction of the house. He had also paid for the final instalment on the lorry, and he had been allowed an easy payment plan on a pick-up which, despite the debts, was essential for transporting coffee, stock and cattle feed as well as the family, but he knew that he could not pay the bank regularly. Waichari recalled now how he had decided not to tell his brother and sister of these problems in case it interfered with their studies.

When he had failed to pay for one of the instalments, the bank had sent him a reminder. The manager had been sympathetic, but he had made it clear that it was his duty to guard public money. Eventually, a notice arrived from an attorney saying that, on behalf of the bank, they wanted him to repay the whole loan this time within three months, or they would have no alternative but to realise their security. Well, Waichari could not raise over ten thousand pounds in that time. The notice had expired the day before. It appeared that they had wasted no time, but gone on to advertise his property for sale by public auction. They had the power too, since they possessed the title deeds.

Waichari had prayed it would not come to this, but it had. He had hoped his brother and sister would not find out about the financial mess; now they had, and they blamed him. What was he supposed to do, paint to them the folly of the old man and then paint himself as the fellow who had done everything to save them? Never. Even now, while he had been lying with the novel on his face, he had been busy thinking as he had never done before. Then his brother and sister had come home from school and disturbed him, not that he blamed them.

'Will you please leave me in peace?' he asked them irritably.

It occurred to him that they wouldn't do that, so he rose to his feet and put on a hat. For a moment he paused to study his sister. After all that weeping, her eyes were red and Waichari could read nothing but hatred in them. He winced inwardly at the injustice of it, and walked out feeling uncomfortable. Outside the simple, L-shaped house, he turned and walked up to the road above the farm. He decided to walk as he thought instead of going for a drive in the pick-up. Once again his mind concentrated on what he had been thinking about all day long. He had to raise eleven thousand pounds in two weeks, but how? Even now he could not think of anything short of a bank robbery. So engrossed was he that he did not notice his sister's friend, Janet, coming from the opposite direction until she murmured some greeting in passing. He acknowledged the greeting and then stopped, surprised that she had passed him without saying a word or two as usual.

'Wait, Janet,' he said. She stopped and he moved to her in his unhurried manner. 'You haven't come to see my sister recently. We miss you.'

'Mother is not feeing well and I am doing all the work at home.'

'I am sorry. I hope she will be better soon.'

'I hope so too.'

The conversation was strained and both of them knew it. Where was her usual human warmth? Waichari asked himself. She must have seen one of the notices, and so was not thinking much of him now. That was a pity for he had grown to like her, and she had been a source of comfort to the family during the past troubled year.

She was an extremely pretty girl of about

eighteen. She had a sleek, oval face and a healthy figure that was almost flawless by Bantu standards. She was the daughter of Mwatha, a farmer across the valley, and she had recently finished her secondary school education.

As his sister's friend, Waichari had always admired Janet's beauty, sympathetic nature and diligence on the farm. Her only flaw was her temper, once it was aroused, which was so unlike her otherwise gentle nature. Now it appeared she could be distant also.

'I have to go now and prepare supper,' she said.

'Why the hurry?' he asked, then added bluntly, 'You must have heard of the misfortune which has overtaken us. I hope it doesn't mean you are going to avoid us in future?'

'How can you say such a thing? I pray to God to give you strength to overcome your problems.' She paused, raised her eyes to his with pity mixed with scorn, and murmured, 'How can you have let it happen so soon? Poor, dear Waitherero. Some guardian you are!' The temper shone from her accusing eyes.

His eyes narrowed and she added hastily, 'Forgive me. I have no right to criticise you. Goodbye.'

She moved on and left him gazing after her with a sickly feeling inside him. She scorned him like his own sister. He had never imagined that Janet Mwatha, of all people, could speak such unpleasant words to him. If she was against him, then the whole world would be also.

He moved on his way, his mind returning to the loan problem, oblivious of the few people and vehicles on the road. He thought of several wild ideas to raise the cash but had to discard them. Finally he concluded it would take a miracle to raise the money in time. Soon he became tired of this aimless walking, climbed the road bank and sat studying the country around. He looked at the hilly land spread out like a map below him, towards Iyego and Weithaga locations. Some people with small incomes were putting up fine houses and driving sleek cars. How did they do it? He knew one who was a civil servant and received bribes; another was a smuggler; another tampered with public funds and still another dealt with the skins of wild animals.

Waichari let out a sigh of relief. Smuggling! Of course, it was the practical solution to his problems. He should have thought of it before. He recalled now how one of his old schoolmates, Njogu, had made a fantastic fortune by smuggling. It was common knowledge that all kinds of people were making fortunes in coffee transactions at the Kenya-Uganda border. It was not the traditional secretive smuggling, but shameless, almost open, smuggling. Waichari threw the cigarette butt away and rose to his feet, thinking about joining the racketeers.

But wait! The business was illegal and he was no criminal. Waichari comforted himself with the thought that top civil servants and police heads were involved. But anyone found to be a contrabandist in Uganda was executed! Waichari convinced himself that he was not squeamish. If someone like Njogu could do it, then so could he.

Still, it was a dirty business, with its incubus of night trips by lake and bush tracks. He hated the idea of careering over the two countries wooing secret deals. He was more used to open transactions.

The more he thought about *magendo* (smuggling), the more he disliked it.

Yet anything was better than losing his home and respect. So he reluctantly decided to give *magendo* a trial.

# Chapter 2

That night, Waichari couldn't sleep. He thought over the decision he had made and, the more he thought about it, the more he disliked it, but he had to choose it or face ruin and humiliation. It was a question of survival, that supreme law of nature. Waichari tried to relax and find sleep, but it did not come easily. He was still uneasy.

When he finally dozed off, he dreamt that he was about to be shot as a smuggler by Ugandan soldiers. It was terribly real. Waichari wanted to scream for mercy as the soldiers levelled the muzzles of their rifles at him and his companions, but he was so terrified that he could not make a sound. There was a terrific explosion and a flash of fire, and as the bullet tore and burned its way into Waichari's chest, he jumped in his bed, then wriggled in confusion. Gradually, he realised that he was only dreaming and sat up shuddering. He cursed his mind for conjuring up such a horrible nightmare, but he asked himself if it wasn't a warning. He decided he had to go ahead, but he would have to be careful. Exhausted by thought, he finally found sleep in the early hours of the morning.

He awoke at nine and, after washing his face and running a comb carelessly through his short hair, he was served tea and buttered toast by a sulking

Waitherero. She did not speak and this suited him. Since there was no turning back, he wanted to think of his line of action. His first course was to enquire from an expert as to how to go about the business. He had to know how much capital was required, where to buy coffee, how to transport it with minimum risk, where to sell it and all that. There was no end to the questions for a beginner like him.

A dozen miles away, at the edge of the mountainous forests in the west, a plump but passably good-looking woman stood looking down on her farm. Two little boys played beside her. She was Jane Ngoju, and she was the envy of the housewives around. She had a bigger and better farm and house than any of them in the cold, tea-growing region and she was the wife of a wealthy man. But Jane was unhappy, for she felt her husband was neglecting her – not materially, but he was with-holding the companionship that is vital to a marriage.

She recalled happier days several years earlier when they were newly married. He never spent weekends in town then, but always came home to share joys, problems and work with her. He had been a bank manager when they got married and she was a primary school teacher. He had been a loving, considerate husband and father, until he developed a mania for investment.

She turned to the two children playing on the grass and some of the cloud in her face lifted. Yes, she still had her sons to kill her loneliness. She called the children and they came running to her. They were aged two and four, and had the dark, healthy and intelligent features of their father. Mrs Njogu picked up the younger of the two and hugged him. It comforted her, for the child was her husband's flesh and blood.

Mrs Njogu went into the kitchen with the children. A few minutes later she heard the sound of an approaching motor vehicle. She came out of the house hopefully, with the children following her but, as the vehicle came closer she could tell it was not the sound of Njogu's Volvo. The vehicle that drove in through the gate was an orange Datsun pick-up. It stopped and a tall, slim young man came out of it, slammed the door and approached her slowly. Her dark, rounded face beamed with genuine pleasure for she did not receive visitors often.

'How are you, Mother of Maina?' he greeted her, lifting his hat with one hand while the other shook her hand.

'I am very well.' She turned to the children. 'Maina! Ngotho! Where are your manners? Greet this uncle.'

Waichari sat on his heels and greeted the children. The older one was at ease but the younger one was shy.

'They are growing into very fine little men indeed,' Waichari remarked. 'Allow me to compliment you sincerely on your excellence as a mother as well as a farmer.'

She ushered him into a large, well-furnished sitting room which he suspected was rarely used. A teenage *ayah* appeared from the kitchen and Mrs Njogu gave her the children and asked her to prepare tea for their guest. She sat opposite Waichari and they talked. Like numerous other rural

14

mothers he had visited, he knew there were few topics she enjoyed more than farming, children and religion.

Presently the *ayah* returned with a tea tray. After pouring the tea she returned to the kitchen. As they sipped, Waichari veered the conversation to the real reason for his visit.

'I have urgent business with your husband,' he said. 'Can you direct me to him?'

Her face darkened with sadness. 'It is not easy,' she said. 'He has so many widespread business interests. At first I was glad, but now I wonder... What is the use of amassing more and more wealth if you don't have time to rest with your children?'

'He is struggling for them, mama. Don't worry, some day he will have time to rest. Where do you suggest I try to find him first?'

'You could try the transport company in Nairobi and his residence after office hours. Ask for Wekesa. He is a young man who has been Njogu's trusted assistant since he started in business. Wekesa always knows his whereabouts. I'll give you the house number and the company's phone number as well.'

'Thank you.'

She rose to her feet, went to a drawer and got a pen and paper. As she wrote it, the older child strayed in.

'I wish I had such a fine little man,' Waichari commented.

Mrs Njogu looked up and smiled. 'You'll be blessed with one some day. Don't worry.' The smile became sad. 'I wish his father would appreciate his blessing, though.' She hesitated, then murmured, 'Waichari, you have been my husband's friend since you were young. If you meet him, please talk to him and convince him that his sons and I miss him. I would be eternally grateful if you could convince him.'

This made Waichari uncomfortable. Who was he to play the role of the elder brother to the big shot? She must be desperate to suggest such a thing. He murmured something about doing what he could.

'Are you going to Father?' the little boy asked him.

'I might,' Waichari replied.

The boy looked straight at Waichari with his clear, dark eyes. 'Tell him I want him to hear me recite the alphabet.'

'I don't believe it,' Waichari said with mock amazement.

'I can.' The boy proceeded to chant from A to Z, making only two mistakes.

'Well done!'

Waichari rose to go. The mother pleaded for him to wait for lunch, but he explained he had much to do. He promised to return after contacting her husband.

As Waichari drove through the cold tea-growing region, he felt sorry for the nice mother and children. Though it was none of his business, he felt compelled to mention their loneliness to Njogu as she had requested, if they met.

'Is it worthwhile seeking out Njogu?' Waichari asked himself. It was certainly a long way to go to ask him about the *magendo* business. Still, there was no harm in calling Njogu's assistant and enquiring about the whereabouts of the big shot. He drove down to Kangema, where his wholesale store was. An elderly man was in charge.

'Are you well, Father of Kambo?' Waichari

greeted him, entering in his unhurried manner. The man nodded his greeting. Waichari went to one of the rooms at the back, where there was a telephone. He produced the paper Mrs Njogu had given him, picked up the phone and turned the handle twice.

'Number, please?' a feminine voice asked.

'Seven zero four zero seven nine, Nairobi.'

'Okay, I'll call you.'


Wekesa put down the telephone receiver and cursed under his breath. This was the third crisis to arise. The problems were too big for him to cope with. Still, they were his responsibilities while the boss was away, and he had to face them.

Wekesa rose from the chair behind the big desk and started pacing about the office. He was a strong young man of medium height, and was well dressed. Right now, however, he was not his usual cheerful self because of the headaches of Njogu Enterprises. Wekesa often wondered if he was competent enough to be Njogu's assistant. This was a job for someone qualified in business adminstration. Njogu himself, being qualified, must have known this, yet he always left matters to Wekesa. Why? Perhaps because they were close to one another, and the big shot trusted him. Wekesa had also helped Njogu build up his business, especially with coffee transactions at the Kenya-Uganda border, where Wekesa came from. They had travelled far together and encountered many adventures...

The telephone bell rang and Wekesa frowned. He hoped there were not more headaches in store for him. He picked the receiver up.

'A call for you from Kangema, Mr Wekesa,' the secretary said. 'It's a man who doesn't give his name but says it's important.'

'It had better be,' Wekesa said. 'Put him through.'

A low, lazy voice came on the line. 'Hello, is that Mr Wekesa?'

'Speaking. What can I do for you?'

'I want to see Mr Njogu. Mrs Njogu has informed me that you can direct me to him. Is he around?'

'No. Who is talking please?'

'Waichari Mathu. Can you tell me where I can find the big man?'

'I'm afraid not. He left here over two weeks ago. Try next week.'

'Next week!' The voice was raised for once. 'I can't wait that long.' There was a long pause and, as Wekesa was about to hang up, the man at the other end seemed to guess it for he said, 'Hang on, please. I was thinking that, since Njogu is away, perhaps you can help me?'

'In what way?'

'Oh! I want advice on a small matter, but I can't discuss it over the phone. I am sure you can handle it as well as the boss. Can I come over?'

'I was just leaving.'

'I could meet you at home. Mrs Njogu gave me the house address. I could be over in two hours. Is it all right?'

Wekesa hesitated. This could be a disturbance, but it could also be a business proposal. Besides, the man sounded as if he was a friend of the boss. 'Okay,' he said. 'Meet me there.'

As Wekesa hung up, he was not too happy about it. He had too much on his mind already, and he didn't want anything more to think about.

Waichari put the phone down slowly. Wekesa had
not sounded very encouraging. He had no choice but
to meet him and try to get the information he
required. Working for Njogu, it was likely that
Wekesa knew all about the coffee racket. Was it
possible to get the information from him?

Waichari returned to the front of the store, told
the keeper he was off to town and would be back in
the evening, and went to the pick-up in his unhurried manner. He got in, engaged gear and drove
down the main street of the town slowly. Soon he
crossed a river and started climbing. The next
sixteen miles meant going up and down hills, round
bends and crossing rivers, through the green, productive land of small farms. The area was well if not
densely populated, and once in a while he passed
small trading centres.

After reaching the district headquarters,
Murang'a, Waichari stopped for petrol, then he
headed for the city. On this road the traffic was
heavier, but the land was less hilly. It was also less
populated and productive. Waichari shifted to fourth
gear and kept pressing the gas pedal slightly all the
way. He tried to relax and enjoy the drive as the
whizzing of the wind drowned out the sound of the
engine while the orange pick-up sped across the land.

Fifty-two miles from Murang'a, he reached the
vast city of Nairobi and drove along the outskirts to
Njogu's town home. It was clean and tolerably quiet.
The flats were first class, if a bit old-fashioned. He
had some difficulty locating the exact number, but
eventually found it. He parked the orange pick-up
outside, like a black car he had seen round the

corner. He got out, slammed the door and approached the gate in his slow motion style. Waichari opened the gate and walked through the flower garden to the massive wood-panelled door and knocked on it.

'Come in,' a voice told him.

He stepped into a spacious, luxuriantly furnished sitting room. Standing by the window was a young man who was shorter and younger than he was. His dark face was rough but pleasant enough.

'Good afternoon,' the young man said in his pleasant voice, offering his hand, which Waichari shook. 'You must be Mr Mathu.'

'Yes, and you, I take it, are Mr Wekesa. I am pleased to meet you. Mrs Njogu spoke well of you.'

'Did she? But don't let us talk standing. Take a seat.'

'Thanks,' Waichari said, sinking on to a divan and stretching his legs.

'When were you with Mrs Njogu?'

'This morning. She gave me a message for her husband. Are you sure you don't know where he is?'

'No. I was telling you the truth when I told you I don't know. I called the depot in Uganda where he supplies goods but was informed he had left.'

'When do you think he will be back?'

'Hard to tell. He has been away for two weeks but he can't take more than three weeks. Are you a friend of his?'

'Yes, we used to go to school together and are of the same age group,' said Waichari. 'He was quite a bright chap. He did better than I and went higher but we never lost contact. We had the same interest in business. Three years ago he suggested I try coffee transactions that had begun in Uganda, as he had done, and again I was not keen.'

Wekesa gave Waichari a sharp look, but the latter, unperturbed, continued, 'Now I wish I had taken his advice. He has prospered while I have got into a financial mess. I am in danger of bankruptcy unless I can raise a considerable sum quickly. I can think of no way except *magendo*. All I wanted is information. Since the boss is away, I thought you could give it to me instead. You've worked with Njogu for a long time now. All I wanted to know is how I am to go about it. Surely it would do no harm if you gave me a hint.'

'I can't...' Wekesa began.

'I know you can't talk about such matters to strangers,' Waichari said, 'but you look intelligent to me. What would I gain by prying into your affairs? Are you going to help me?'

Wekesa kept studying Waichari's face and then shook his head slightly. Waichari rose to his feet in his slow motion manner.

'All right,' he said, 'I understand. I'll try someone else. Sorry to waste your time.'

'Wait!' Wekesa said. He started pacing around the room, thinking hard. He seemed to come to a conclusion and turned to Waichari.

'One cannot talk freely about such matters to everybody,' he said, 'but you seem genuine and I don't want to offend you. I don't see any harm, either. What do you want to know about *magendo*?'

Waichari was surprised. Wekesa had obviously been reluctant to confide. What had made him change his mind so suddenly? Anyway, it did not matter as long as he got the information he wanted.

'Everything there is to know about it,' he replied in answer to Wekesa's question. 'Start from the beginning, how it began.'

'It started when Amin declared the "Economic War" and expelled the Asians in 1972,' Wekesa began without much enthusiasm. 'You know how Ugandan commerce and industry were taken over by ignorant people, and how Amin's economic dream turned into an economic nightmare. Prices in Uganda have rocketed to an unbelievable extent, the shilling is very weak and there is an acute shortage of essential commodities. Ugandan farmers, therefore, prefer to sell their crops in Kenya and get paid for them in Kenyan currency. That way they can buy the badly needed foodstuffs here. In Uganda, the government is solely responsible for the sales. You can guess how poor a bargain the growers get. Sometimes they complain they get nothing at all, when their coffee is exchanged for small arms from Europe. The same arms are used by Amin's trigger-happy soldiers in their usual exercise of eliminating rebels.'

Wekesa smiled. He was beginning to warm to the topic which was, in fact, his favourite. 'Before we proceed, I'll mention briefly the type of coffee you'll be handling. Uganda grows mostly "Robusta", while Kenya's is mostly the "Arabica", which fetches higher prices on the world market. Kenya is also one of the few African countries which grows the "Columbian Mild". This type of coffee is even better and is mostly grown in Central and South America. That is why when Brazilian coffee spoiled, the demand for and the prices of our coffee became higher. So you can see that even if the Ugandan

"Robusta" is of high quality, we cannot mix it with ours. I mean we can't do our crop much good by mixing it up with that of Uganda. But if the big shots don't mind, why should we?'

'What kind of big shots are involved?' asked Waichari.

Wekesa gestured at Waichari's ignorance with an exclamation. Then he lowered his voice and explained that, apart from ordinary people and policemen, there were top customs and excise department officials, civil servants, district commissioners and MPs. He went so far as to mention a few police chiefs and even a provincial commissioner or two.

Waichari raised his eyebrows which was his mild way of showing surprise.

'Now tell me how to go about the racket. Where and how to buy the stuff.'

'You'll find the buyers and sellers in Chepkube, on the Kenyan side of the border. It is the centre of negotiations. Politicians call it the notorious Black Gold City,' Wekesa said, grinning. He was relaxed now and the information was flowing freely. 'Smugglers' paradise,' he added.

Waichari asked, 'How much profit am I to expect per bag? I hope it is not less than a hundred shillings?'

Wekesa gave another exclamation and made another gesture at Waichari's ignorance. 'A hundred! This is black gold. You'll buy it at three to six hundred shillings per bag. You'll divide that bag into four portions, and sell each portion for over one thousand shillings! That is a profit of over four thousand shillings per bag!'

Waichari got to his feet, excited. 'My lorry can

hold over one hundred bags. That is over four hundred thousand shillings profit on each trip! I could clear a staggering loan I have in less than three trips! I would surely save my farm and store from being auctioned. It is too good to be true!'

'It is, though a certain percentage must be kept aside to bribe the police and customs officials at the border, unless you prefer secret trips by boat or by land, using unpatrolled but difficult routes.'

'How much do you suggest I start with?'

'With a single lorry, I would suggest about fifty thousand shillings.'

'But I don't have that kind of money right now. I could raise about ten thousand shillings.'

'Oh,oh!' exclaimed Wekesa, disappointed. 'I thought that at least you could raise that much. You mention you have a store. What kind of store?'

'A wholesale store of general goods.'

'Excellent. Can you get a good quantity of sugar? The Ugandans regard it as white gold just as we regard their coffee as black gold.'

'I can get a little... worth about another ten thousand shillings.'

'Good!' said Wekesa, brightening. 'Add commodities like flour, salt, fat and soap and they will serve. After all, the Ugandans need Kenyan currency in order to buy these commodities. You would make double profit by crossing the border loaded with white gold and returning loaded with black gold.'

'Thanks for the tip. You've been very helpful, but can you give me any more details? Like handling the police and trigger-happy soldiers?'

'I will give you more information tomorrow, if you will give me your address and telephone number. I'll contact you tomorrow, at eleven in the morning. We have some workers from Njogu's area whom I want to question about you. If they confirm you really are Njogu's friend, I don't see why I shouldn't accompany you to Uganda and help you in any way I can. You see, I too want to go there on other matters. Now will you give me that number and address?'

'Would you really accompany me?' Waichari asked in disbelief. 'I'd really appreciate it.'

He wrote down his full address and phone number and gave it to Wekesa. 'You can ask your men and one or two of them ought to confirm what I say. You'd do better still if you contacted Mrs Njogu herself.'

Waichari got to his feet. 'I've got to go now; it's getting late. Thanks a lot. I'll be waiting for your call.'

Wekesa escorted Waichari to the gate where they shook hands. Waichari walked to his pick-up slowly, got in and drove off. There were only two vehicles in the lane, but he did not speed. As he went round a corner, he noticed that the big, black car he had seen on his arrival was still parked there. He could not see the occupants clearly, but he felt they were watching him. They probably didn't think much of people who drove round town in pick-ups.

Waichari dismissed them from his mind and concentrated on his conversation with Wekesa. He thought it had been a very instructive interview. Wekesa was certainly worth knowing and he hoped they would go together. Since Waichari was so ignorant about *magendo,* it would pay to have an expert with him.

But wait! Wekesa had been reluctant to part with

the information at first. Now he had gone so far as to offer his assistance. How could he after so short an acquaintance? There had to be a catch. But what? Waichari could think of none. He concluded it was just a kind offer to help a friend of his boss, since he was also going to Uganda. After all, Wekesa wanted to check on Waichari's relations with his boss.

After skirting the city, Waichari put the pick-up into top gear and sped across the semi-flat grass-land. It was nearly evening. All he had to do now was to wait for Wekesa's call. If he offered to accompany him, then Waichari's way was clear, but if Wekesa refused to go with him, he would go alone and learn all he had to know in Chepkube itself. He could not afford to waste time.

# Chapter 3

After reaching his small home town, Waichari stopped at his wholesale store. He ordered the elderly storekeeper to stand by for stocktaking early next morning, even though it was a Sunday. He also left instructions for the crew of the lorry not to take the day off as usual, but to be ready to have it serviced as early as possible. He had decided to get on the move the following night, with or without Wekesa.

Having left these instructions, Waichari drove home. He felt he had spent the day well, but there was trouble in store for him when he reached home. He parked the pick-up in its shed nearby and walked to the house. He pushed open the front door and entered the dining room. It was nearly eight pm and the lamps had been lit. Muna was pacing about the room restlessly.

'Hello, Waichari. Where have you been?'

'Disco dancing,' Waichari replied shortly. 'Tell Waitherero I need a hot bath.'

Muna went to carry out the order and then returned. He went to the window and stood looking out into the night. Waichari went to his room, got a fresh towel and clothes and returned to the dining-room.

Presently a girl with short Afro hair, a sleek oval face and a brown dress came in and announced the bath was ready. Waichari raised his eyebrows in surprise. It was not his sister who had come to announce the bath was ready, but her friend, Janet Waruguru.

Normally it was not surprising to see her around the house helping his sister with household chores, but he had not expected to see her after she had expressed so much scorn for him the day before. 'Some guardian you are!' she had said. He could tell by her impersonal attitude that she still didn't think much of him.

'Hello, Waruguru,' he greeted her. 'Don't think I am complaining, but how come you are doing my sister's work?'

'She asked me to,' Janet replied, 'for she is not feeling well. She will be all right. Don't let it make you let the water grow cold.'

Waichari was worried and he hoped Waitherero was not really sick; as if they didn't have enough troubles already. After a hasty bath, he returned to the dining-room where Janet served him and Muna chicken with potatoes and pumpernickels.

'Have you got any idea what is wrong with Waitherero?' Waichari asked Muna after Janet had returned to the kitchen.

'I'm afraid it's all my fault,' Muna replied after some hesitation. 'After seeing to the cattle I thought I would go to town and play a record or two on the juke box this afternoon. As I was leaving, a friend of mine who was coming out of a bar noticed me and hurried across the street to me. He told me that he had overheard a conversation in the backroom of the bar between the bank manager and Mr Kanyi, the Tea Society chairman. They were discussing the sale

28

of our property. It appears Kanyi is determined to buy it. He wants both the farm and the store at any cost, and asked if arrangements could be made to sell them together. I felt sick all the way home. Waitherero noticed my gloom and pressed me to tell her. I shouldn't have repeated what I heard to her, and I am sorry. You know her. She was so upset that when Janet dropped in on her way home, she had to stay and soothe her.'

Waichari rose to his feet, having lost his appetite. He lit a cigarette automatically and stood puffing. 'That big mongoose's dream of buying our heritage must be shattered.'

'Have you got a plan?'

'More or less. But as there is no way you can help, don't trouble your head over it.'

The girls came into the room. Slim young Waitherero passed on into her room, avoiding looking at Waichari. This auction business was proving more nightmarish than he expected. His sister hated him and Janet scorned him; not that he blamed them. He could hardly bear it when Janet, avoiding looking directly at him as Waitherero had done, looked at Muna and spoke.

'I've got to go now. Will you please escort me home?'

'I want to breathe fresh air, Janet,' Waichari said. 'I'll escort you.'

'Thank you,' she said coldly. 'You can accompany Muna and I.'

'Let me have the privilege, will you, brother?' asked Waichari.

'If you wish it,' Muna said.

'But I don't...' Janet began. Waichari guessed she

29

was about to say that she didn't wish it, and he hastily interrupted her. 'I know, I know – you don't like to be kept waiting. Let's go.'

She was about to protest again when he silenced her with a stern look. She let him lead her into the night. Once they were on one of the fenced paths that were between the small farms, however, he had a taste of one of her bursts of bad temper, which spoilt her almost perfect character.

'I don't see why you are bothering yourself,' she said.

'I wanted to talk to you.'

'I don't see anything important for us to discuss.'

He was moving at his usual slow pace, but she was moving faster ahead of him despite the darkness. There was a moon, but it was hidden by clouds. He noticed that she was moving out of the range of the beam of light thrown by the flashlight he carried. 'Won't you slow down? There are some nasty gullies dug by torrents ahead, and you could break a leg.'

'I know every inch of this route, with or without light.'

Waichari could hardly believe his ears. He recalled how Janet had always been polite and friendly to him whenever she came to visit his sister. In fact, he could have sworn she liked him.

As a junior secondary school student, the little, shy Janet would stop at his home first, with her heavy trunk, whenever they were given school holidays. She had also made it a habit to drop in on her way to church. At around sixteen years of age, after overcoming her shyness with him, she would come in her Sunday best and meet him outside the house, polishing his shoes or something. There she would linger on, talking to him in her soft voice.

She had often worked on his farm, and he and his family had often worked on hers too, digging or picking coffee. Whenever they were picking coffee, she would somehow make her way to the trees he was picking, seeming to enjoy conversing with him more than with the boys of her own age who always pursued her.

She had proved invaluable after the tragedy that had robbed him of his parents. He didn't know how they would have managed without her. She was seventeen then, but her words of comfort were like those of a grown-up person. Sincere words that came from her heart, for she had made their tragedy hers too.

That was the Janet he had grown to know and like. That was why he could not believe she could be so rude to him now, as he escorted her home. He had got so used to her warmth that he could not bear her coldness towards him; that was why he had offered to escort her, hoping to coax her back into friendliness. Now he could see it was not going to be easy. Whether she knew the route or not, she was forced to slow down by the gullies he had mentioned and he caught up with her.

'Steady,' he warned, 'there is a hole there. You don't want to break a leg.'

'Why should you care?' she said, turning to look at him. She shouldn't have done that, for she stepped into the hole and stumbled. Waichari's hand shot out and caught and steadied her before she could fall. They stopped, and he remained gripping her hand. Her oval face was faintly illuminated by the moon, which was now only half hidden by the clouds.

31

'Because I would like to take care of you,' he said impulsively, in answer to her question. It was a blunder on his part, for she laughed sarcastically and said, 'Take care of me! Having failed to take care of your own affairs, how can you take care of someone else?'

He winced inwardly and let go of her hand. She stumbled on down the slope and he followed. Presently they cleared the slope and the moon became brighter. She was able to move faster and leave him behind with his customary slow walk.

Then she stopped and waited for him to catch up with her. He was surprised until he saw the reason why. There was a gang of teenagers seated beside the path ahead, three on each side. They stood up and came to the middle of the path as Waichari came on with his slow, assured step, the girl behind him. Recognising Waichari and knowing that he was not the type of man to trifle with, they stood aside and let him and the girl pass unmolested.

'There, I am glad I came with you,' he said, 'but I am also sad because you are cruel to me, Waruguru. I can hardly believe it of you. How can you?'

'Because you have disappointed me,' she said. At least his action of protecting her from the teenage gang had thawed her enough to enable her to talk to him. 'You have disgraced yourself publicly and brought suffering to Waitherero and Muna. Now it is my turn to ask how you did it. How did it happen?'

'It was unforeseen and unavoidable, Waruguru. It happened through no fault of my own.'

'How can you expect me to believe that? How can one not foresee trouble when one borrows a sum beyond one's income? Anyhow, what are you going to do now and where are you going to take your family?'

'For the present, I am going on a journey tomorrow to try to raise the cash.'

'I am glad to hear that. Try your level best to raise it and to avoid such pitfalls in future. As for me, I am considering going for a secretarial course in Nyeri.'

'We would be very sorry to lose you,' he said, and meant it. 'You have been our pillar of strength since our mother went. I was hoping you could keep my sister company while I am away.'

'I will until I depart.'

They had reached her home. 'Thank you for escorting me. So long.' She made for her gate without even shaking hands when he called after her, 'Try and come in the afternoon and say goodbye to me, will you?'

She paused and then called over her shoulder, 'I might.' She walked through the small gate of her home and disappeared. Waichari walked home slowly, feeling he had lost something valuable, an inexhaustible source of human warmth. On reaching home he found Muna had gone to his room. He went to bed as well and tried to read, but he found concentration as difficult as the night before. He kept wondering if Wekesa would accompany him, and what lay ahead. But what disturbed him most was Janet's hostility.

'I shan't lose sleep over a woman,' he said to himself, and fell into a troubled sleep. An oval face, with a smooth, dark brown complexion, clear expressive eyes, a blunt nose and a small mouth, came before him. It was crowned by short Afro hair. The face was filled with scorn, especially in the expressive eyes. The mouth spoke, and the voice was also filled with scorn: 'Having failed to take care of your own affairs, how can you take care of someone else?'


Kimani wa Mbogo tugged at his blanket and covered his head, trying to prolong the sweet morning sleep. He was in one of the rooms of a block on one of the low income estates of Nairobi. The single room served as bedroom, sitting room, nursery, kitchen and store, all rolled into one. Kimani was finding it difficult to sleep on because his two 'sub-tenants' were chatting and laughing loudly and his wife was also making noise clattering dishes and scolding her children. The biggest din of all came from outside where everyone shared a common verandah.

Kimani wa Mbogo uncovered his head, raised it, pulled aside the light sheet serving as a curtain and yelled, 'Shut up all of you, will you? I am the master of this house, and I deserve some respect.'

His 'sub-tenants' and his wife fell silent and Kimani covered his head again. This was much better! If only the racket was not louder than usual outside... but presently his wife hurried in, came up to him and whispered, 'There is a man asking for you. People are refusing to show him our house in case he is a policeman.'

'Policeman!' Kimani gasped, jumping out of bed. Wearing only his underpants, he peeped round the door. He was a slim, dark man with lean features, shaggy hair and a moustache. He swiftly slipped into trousers and a shirt.

'That is my boss!' he cried in alarm. 'Look at the

house, you dirty hyena of a woman! It is like a manure pit! What can the boss want? He must have discovered I pinched four tins of paint from a client! He must have come to investigate. I am ruined!' Kimani looked around the room in panic. 'Come in!' he called nervously.

The door opened, but the unwelcome guest did not come in.

'Good morning,' Wekesa said in the doorway. 'I wanted to see you, Kimani. Come outside with me.'

Kimani followed him out of the filthy block to a white, Ford saloon car which was parked in the lane outside. Wekesa got into the back seat and gestured to Kimani to do the same. Nervously, Kimani obeyed.

'You come from a location called Iyego, Kangema division,' Wekesa began. 'Ever heard of a fellow called Waichari Mathu?'

The question was totally unexpected and it was some moments before the relief sank in, dispelling Kimani's fear of being sacked. He replied, 'Yes, sir, he is well known. Firstly, because of his father, who served as an example of diligence. Secondly, because Waichari knows his way around.'

'Answer properly,' Wekesa snapped. 'What kind of diligence does the father show?'

'Showed... He died last year. There was a big funeral. He used to work here, but he went to settle down in the country at the beginning of the sixties. He didn't have much, but he became well-established in business and farming.'

'What kind of property did he leave?'

'There is a plot with a wholesale shop and rooms for hire. There is also a lorry, but what is most impressive is the farm. Students of the agricultural school used to visit it when their mother was alive.'

'Don't tell me the mother is dead, too?'

'They died together in a motor accident. It was in the newspaper.'

'That's terrible. How big is the lorry?'

'Nine or ten tons.'

'Now tell me about Waichari. What kind of man is he?'

'I don't know him all that well. All I know of him is that he is generous, quiet, likes girls and is hard working.'

'Are you trying to make me believe he is all that nice?'

'He is reckless – like opening his shop when others are closed on National days. He is also dangerous if provoked. He crippled someone who stoned him during the last Parliamentary campaigns, and he cut the arm of one of three robbers who broke into their store while he and his father were sleeping in it.'

'I can believe that. But has he had any criminal convictions?'

'Not that I know of.'

'Do you know where he went to school?'

'Yes, Muguru Primary School and then Njiri's High School.'

'Would you know if he is a friend of Mr Njogu?'

'No, but it is likely.'

'Have you heard of any financial embarrassment concerning him?'

'No. In our area we would regard him as rich. I don't see how...'

'That is all. Thanks for your time.' Wekesa produced a pound note and gave it to Kimani, much to the latter's delight, since he had expected trouble. 'Buy the children some milk.'

'Thank you, sir,' Kimani said, getting out of the car.

He watched the car drive off, wondering what all the fuss over Waichari was all about.

Wekesa struck the main road, headed for home and accelerated. He was going over his conversation with Kimani. Further down the road, behind a lorry, a big black car started up and followed Wekesa's at a distance. He did not notice it, and he had not noticed it following him on his way there.


Waichari went over the list in his mind and a smile flickered over his hard features. Thanks to a good year, he still had some stock left despite the loan repayment. He had come early in the morning, left the mechanics working and had come to help the old man with the stock-taking. This had not taken very long since it was a wholesale store without much variety or quantity of goods, but what he had was enough to add up to a little over thirty-two thousand shillings. Cash money was short of his expectations – a mere seven thousand shillings. He was eleven thousand short of the estimate Wekesa had suggested, but nothing would stop him now.

The telephone bell rang and Waichari snapped out of his musings. He picked it up and looked at his watch simultaneously. He saw it was a few minutes after eleven. He could hardly believe Wekesa had kept his word, if it was him.

'Hello, this is Wekesa speaking. I have decided to

accompany you. Can you be ready by tonight?'

'To tell you the truth, I have already started the preparations.'

'How much stock do you have?'

'Worth thirty-two thousand, plus seven thousand in cash.'

'Not bad. Come with the lorry at midnight. Remember to bring as many empty sacks as possible. It would also be advisable to have some sort of weapon.'

'What about manpower?'

'Three or four will do. You can hire extra help after getting there if necessary.'

'Anything else?'

'An escort saloon car will be necessary; you can use mine, but don't forget a blanket or two. The place is cold! Tell you more when we meet. See you.'

Waichari hung up, feeling glad that he would have someone to guide him. But he could not help wondering again why Wekesa was offering to do so much after such a brief acquaintance.

Later that morning there was the sound of a powerful engine coming to a stop in front of the store. Waichari went out. It was the lorry. The driver, a middle-aged, quiet, but tough-looking man, came out of the driving cab, followed by two ragged turn-boys.

'Is it okay, Mutua?' Waichari asked the driver, who nodded affirmatively.

'Excellent. Come to my office, the three of you.'

Waichari asked the storekeeper to bring them tea and samosas and, as they ate, he listened to their adventures on the last trip, which had taken them to the deserts of the North-Eastern Region to fetch cattle. They had many stories to tell.

'I am afraid we have a more dangerous journey ahead,' he said. They fell silent and listened keenly to him. 'You know I am in financial difficulties. They have compelled me to take desperate measures. I am about to undertake *magendo*.'

The two boys listened more eagerly but the more mature Mutua was uneasy. 'What kind of *magendo*?' he asked.

'The coffee racket at the Kenya-Uganda border. It is a dangerous and dirty business. He who comes with me must do so at personal risk. I am not going to force anyone, but I would be grateful for volunteers now and in the future. The work will be harder but, for the risk and extra work, for each day of the mission, the pay will be five times higher than usual. Think it over and let me know your decision.' Waichari left them to decide and went to the storekeeper at the front to ask for the stock money.

'I am very sorry, Father of Kambo, but we are closing down the shop until further notice.' Waichari said, avoiding looking at the man's distressed face. 'I am taking all the stock except the maize, beans, potatoes and animal feed. Sell them all as quickly as possible, close the shop and go and work on the farm until I return.'

'Yes sir,' the man said gloomily. 'I understand.'

Waichari stuffed the pockets of his jacket with the seven thousand shillings and returned to the back room.

'Who is coming with me?' he asked.

'We two are,' one of the boys replied.

Waichari turned to the brooding Mutua inquiringly.

'I don't like it,' he said. 'I've got a wife and children back home in Kangundo, but I cannot forsake Mathu's son in his hour of need. So I am going to come.'

'Thanks, all of you. We're taking most of this stock with us, and I want it to be loaded immediately. Mutua, why don't you park the lorry in position?'

Mutua went to position the lorry and they all got to work, carrying the sacks and packages to the lorry. It was tiring work which took several hours. When it was over they were all exhausted and hungry.

'Buy yourselves two kilos of beef and one bottle of beer each,' Waichari said, giving Mutua two pounds. 'Then take a rest until ten pm when I expect you to come with the lorry and collect me at home.'

Having completed these arrangements, Waichari drove home in the pick-up to eat and prepare his personal belongings. It was three pm and he hoped Janet would be there.

For the first time since Friday, Waitherero seemed to be willing to talk to him as she served him food.

'Janet dropped in on her way from church,' she said. 'She told me to tell you that she couldn't wait, but to tell you goodbye and good luck on your journey.'

At least Janet had not ignored him altogether, Waichari thought, with a little relief.

'I didn't know you were going away,' Waitherero went on. 'Where are you going?'

'On a long, fund-raising safari,' Waichari replied. 'If you could take care of the home and stop being bitter at me, it would help a lot.'

'How can I help being bitter?'

'Bitterness won't help, little sister. Just hold your peace and hope for the best.'

After the meal Waichari went to his room to pack. He included a sword, as Wekesa had said he should have a weapon. After that, he lay down to rest. An hour later, he was disturbed by Muna and Waitherero's voices. They sounded upset.

'Yes, it's him!' Muna said. 'He is determined. Others are just watching from behind the fence, but he has come right in. He has gone too far.'

'He'll kick us out and we'll be like vagrants,' Waitherero said tearfully.

As they went on talking, Waichari swung his legs off the bed and went to the dining-room. Muna and Waitherero were at the window. It was apparent they were discussing a huge, pot-bellied man in a faded grey suit who was standing at the top of the farm, surveying the land. It was Kanyi, the Tea Society chairman, whose conversation with the bank manager had upset Waitherero the day before.

'Ah!' Waichari breathed with narrowed eyes. He went out of the house and walked up to Kanyi in his unhurried manner. Kanyi was disconcerted by Waichari's menacing air.

'Good afternoon,' Waichari said, 'what can I do for you?'

'I am just watching the countryside,' said Kanyi. Surprisingly, Kanyi's voice, despite his bulk, was like that of a girl.

'Well, would you mind finding another viewpoint? The farther away it is from here, the better.'

'It has been publicly announced that this property can be viewed, mister.'

41

'Perhaps, but you haven't bought it yet and don't you forget it.'

'We shall see about that,' Kanyi sneered.

'Yes, we shall see,' Waichari agreed quietly, accepting the challenge. 'In the meantime, go away and stay away.'

With that, he turned back to the house. Kanyi stood looking after him, swore under his breath, went to a station wagon parked on the road and drove away. He could hardly wait to buy the property and get the pleasure of kicking Waichari out.

Waichari returned to bed, dismissed Kanyi from his mind and lay brooding over Janet and the journey ahead. He eventually dozed off, to be shaken awake by Muna hours later. The room was pitch dark.

'You are wanted by the crew of the lorry,' Muna said urgently.

'Wanted? Crew?' Waichari muttered in confusion. As realisation dawned on him, he groped for his shoes in the darkness. After slipping them on, he picked up his suitcase and hat and went to the dining-room. Waitherero studied him, her face worried.

'Please be careful,' she said, as if she had a feeling it was not a normal trip.

Waichari smiled at her reassuringly, and gave her a five pound note. 'Keep this for necessities. See that work goes on as usual. The coffee should be weeded and the milk must be delivered on time.'

Waichari walked out with Waitherero and Muna followed. Mutua was waiting outside and they all walked up to the big lorry which was parked near the pick-up. The turn-boys were in the cab. Mutua climbed on to the driving seat while Waichari shook hands with his brother and sister. The moon was bright and they could see one another clearly.

'We do wish you luck,' Muna said. 'It is only twelve days to the auction bell.'

'I know.' He opened the cab door and paused to ask Waitherero, 'Say goodbye to Waruguru for me, will you?'

She nodded, and Waichari climbed into the cab with his case and slammed the door. Mutua started the engine and the big lorry moved slowly forward, round the spacious parking lot and through the wooden gate on to the main road. After striking the main road, it accelerated further away until it disappeared round a bend. Waichari had joined the great rush for black gold.

# Chapter 4

'I am afraid we are being followed,' Wekesa told
Waichari. They were in Wekesa's white Ford car on
the road from Nairobi to Nakuru. Wekesa was
driving and the car was speeding across plains thick
with grass and shrubs. Behind them, Mutua, driving
the lorry, was following the car closely. It was 1.30
am and there was little traffic on the road.

Waichari had arrived at Njogu's residence punc-
tually at midnight. He had left Mutua and the boys
in the lorry and gone into the house where he had
found Wekesa packing. Waichari asked what kind of
business was taking Wekesa to Uganda. Wekesa
had explained he wanted to hold talks with his boss
over the business. This suited Waichari, since he
wanted to meet Njogu also and deliver his family's
message and perhaps even borrow a little capital
from the big shot.

After that, they had driven off and Waichari had
relaxed, trying to enjoy the journey, until Wekesa
had commented that they were being followed.
Waichari turned his head sharply. Apart from the
lorry, there were only two other vehicles behind
them. They were just over a mile behind.

'Which vehicle do you think is following us?'

'The one which is directly behind the lorry. Note
that we are doing fifty kilometres per hour to enable

the lorry to keep pace with us. Other saloon cars are overtaking us with ease. But this one doesn't. I can't see why it should be so slow. See, he is already being overtaken by another car. I think it's better if we can take no chances. Hang on.'

Wekesa pressed the accelerator pedal to the floor-board. The car shot forward, leaving the lorry behind. Not knowing what was going on, Mutua accelerated the lorry also as Wekesa had known he would. They kept up the high speed across the shrub-land despite the potholes in the road. Waichari noticed that the car behind them had increased speed also. After six kilometres or so, Wekesa finally slowed down again, and Mutua was relieved to do the same. The car behind them also slowed down.

'See what I mean?' Wekesa asked Waichari. 'I wonder who he is and what he wants. It can't be the police since we haven't started smuggling yet. It could be crooks planning a hi-jack or something. You must have read about them in the newspapers.'

'You could be right,' Waichari said, suddenly grim. He thought for a moment and then told Wekesa to stop the car.

'I am curious to see their reaction,' he said, 'and if they try to do anything, we'll be ready.'

'Right,' Wekesa said, slowing the car down to a halt.

Swiftly, Waichari grabbed his suitcase from the back seat and removed his sword. 'I am glad I followed your advice and carried a weapon. What about you?'

'I have one also,' Wekesa said. He unlocked the glove compartment and removed an evil-looking pistol.

'Wha—a—at?' Waichari couldn't help exclaiming in surprise.

'They are coming,' Wekesa explained. 'We've got to move quickly. We could pretend to have a mechanical problem. Tell your crew to stay in the lorry. We shouldn't look as if we are waylaying them.'

It had slowed down. Whoever was driving it was uncertain of what to do. It was only half a mile behind. Then it accelerated and came towards them. It whizzed past them like an arrow. All they could see was that it was a big black car, with two or three men in it. Waichari claimed it looked familiar, though he could not remember where he had seen it.

'I can't see why anyone would be interested in us,' Wekesa said.

'Me neither. Anyway, since we've been forewarned, we'll keep a sharp lookout for them.'

They moved onwards past the town and lake Naivasha, and across a vast plain dotted with acacia trees. They saw nothing more of the black car and concluded that the crooks had given up.

But near Nakuru, they came across a police road block, complete with spikes and rifles.

'Oh, oh!' Wekesa said nervously, halting behind a trailer which was being inspected. 'We're in trouble.'

Mutua pulled up behind them. The trailer was allowed to pass on and two of the policemen came to Wekesa's car and glared at him and Waichari. They inspected the licence on the windscreen and the tyres.

'Brakelights,' snapped the younger policeman.

Wekesa pressed the brake pedal; the lights worked.

'Signals!'

Wekesa turned on the signals.

'Put on the handbrake.'

Wekesa did so. The policeman pushed the car hard and it shifted a foot. 'Park the car on the side for booking!' snapped the young officer.

'It was working last evening,' Wekesa explained.

'Park the car aside for booking, *sokwe!* (chimpanzee)' the officer shouted angrily.

While he wrote, the other officer, a corporal, inspected the lorry and its cargo. Seeing Mutua was in trouble, Waichari went to the lorry.

'You're taking these goods to Uganda,' said the corporal.

'We're taking them to Nakuru,' Waichari told him.

'Shut up! I know a *magendo* consignment when I see one. People like you should be hanged for smuggling foodstuff out of the country, leaving the masses hungry.'

'That is a wild and baseless accusation,' Waichari said, slipping a hundred shillings into the corporal's hand. The officer glared at him, but he let them proceed on their way.

In Nakuru town, Waichari decided they should rest themselves and the engines a while, so they looked for a place to stay. They found a night club with a hotel-cum-bar on the ground floor, and lodgings and a disco upstairs. As the lights and the music were welcoming, they parked the vehicles in the parking lot and entered the hotel. They took seats and a sleepy waitress served them light meals and drinks.

Unfortunately for them, there was a squad of policemen terrorising the town in those days. A jeepload of them came storming into the motel as if on a raid. They were all vicious-looking young men wearing black boots, light green trousers, combat jackets and black berets. A few of them had guns.

'Oh, no!' Wekesa cried in horror. 'Did it have to happen while we're here? Whatever happens, Waichari, don't argue with them.'

'Who are they?'

'They are from a special, utterly ruthless police force who call themselves the *Ngorokos*. They are being trained to tackle cattle rustlers,' Wekesa lowered his voice, 'but they beat up, rape and even kill innocent people. They also escort contraband coffee convoys from Uganda to the coast, at a price, of course. It is alleged that there is a group of powerful people behind them.'

The *Ngorokos* swooped down on the other side of the room and started yelling, demanding ID cards. Here and there a slap rang out and someone was slammed against the wall. Furniture was overturned during the violence

'They are deliberately terrorising the patrons to force the proprietor to quit,' Wekesa whispered fearfully. 'The officer with them wants the property.'

The officer looked around the room. Waichari's group caught his interest and he walked over to them, glass in hand.

'You are gangsters,' he stated.

'We are businessmen,' Wekesa protested. 'I am the assistant manager of Njogu Enterprises, and these men are members of the transport crew.'

'You look more like an alien to me, and a very ugly one at that,' the officer told Wekesa.

'I am purely Kenyan,' said Wekesa, producing his ID and job cards.

48

The officer did not take them, but poured his drink on their heads and then smashed the glass against the wall. Satisfied with his insane display of authority, he walked away and led most of his gang of bullies upstairs, where the music had already stopped.

'Let's get out of here before I am tempted to commit murder,' Waichari hissed in fury, wiping the whisky from his face.

They paid their bill and walked out. It was a relief to get out of the town and on to the main road to Kitale.

They went through a fertile wheat and maize growing area, then entered Molo plains which were suitable for cattle and sheep. After leaving the junction to Kisumu, they came across more wheat fields, then entered the forest area. As dawn began to break Wekesa discomforted Waichari by declaring they were being followed again.

'I think it is the same car, but they are being more cautious this time. They are driving with their lights off and they are keeping a greater distance,' Wekesa told him.

As the light became clearer, Waichari could make out the black car, about two miles behind them. 'You're right. They are beginning to get on my nerves. We'll have to have a talk with them.'

'Yes, but I don't see how we can manage it. They could be dangerous.' They discussed the problem for a while and finally they agreed on an ambush for lack of a better plan. After going round a bend – out of the sight of the pursuing car – they increased speed to put as great a distance as possible between them. Then, after going round a sharp bend, they made sure that no other vehicle was in sight and brought their vehicles to a halt. Waichari ran to the lorry and parked it across the road, blocking it. He explained the situation to his bewildered crew as he did so. They went to hide in the forest on Waichari's instructions.

Waichari and Wekesa hid close to the place where the black car was most likely to stop, at the top of the road bank, so that the road was beneath them.

The big black car came speeding round the bend. When the driver saw the lorry blocking the road, he stepped sharply on the brake, making the car swerve dangerously with a squeal of tortured tyres. It stopped just in time to avoid smashing into the rear of the lorry. Instantly, the driver slammed the car into reverse gear while his companion whipped out a gun.

At the same time, Wekesa aimed and fired his gun, making recoil in his hand with an ear-splitting explosion. One of the rear tyres of the black car blew up and it came to a halt. A wild shot answered from the car. Waichari and Wekesa fell flat on the ground.

'What did you do that for?' Waichari whispered angrily. 'Someone could easily get killed! Besides, more traffic will be here soon.'

Wekesa ignored Waichari and shouted in Kiswahili, 'You are surrounded. Come out with your hands up. We don't want to hurt you but will if you disobey.' He fired a warning shot, shattering a window, and then repeated the message in slow, clear English.

After a while, two tall, pitch black men in plain suits came out of the car with their hands up, just as the sound of an approaching bus was heard.

'We've got to move fast,' Wekesa told Waichari as they came out of their hiding place and down the road bank. 'Order your men to drive on while we take these crooks off the road.'

'Right.' Waichari raised his voice and shouted, 'Mutua, remove the lorry from here at once and await us further on.'

Closer and closer came the sound of the bus. Mutua and the boys ran to the lorry while Wekesa and Waichari approached the gangsters. Wekesa kept his gun pointed at them while Waichari searched them for weapons. One of the gangsters had a gun in his pocket, which Waichari duly pointed at them, though he didn't know how to use it.

'This be outrage,' one of the gangsters, the fatter of the two began. 'You is got no right to...'

'Shut up and get off the road!' Wekesa snarled, ramming the muzzle of his gun into the back of the gangster.

Mutua managed to drive away, but Wekesa and Waichari had to practically shove the gangsters off the road and into the forest before the bus appeared. It was big and white with a black stripe, and belonged to the Overseas Touring Company Ltd. The bus slowed down as it came across Wekesa's white car and the gangster's blue one. The driver seemed to conclude they had been involved in a minor accident, then he accelerated away.

Fifty metres or so into the forest, Waichari ordered the gangsters to stop and turn, so that they faced the muzzles of the guns.

'All right, start talking. For a start, tell me who you are and why you were following us.'

The two men just stared at Waichari stonily.

'They are hard core,' Wekesa said. 'We haven't time to play around. Check if they have IDs.'

A quick search revealed they had none. Just money, handkerchiefs, keys and receipts. Waichari thought for a moment, then he grinned wickedly. 'We'll sabotage their car and take all their money.'

Wekesa grinned also. 'Imagine being left in the middle of nowhere without transport or money!' he said, pocketing the cash.

They walked back to the road and to the gangsters' car. They searched the car and found nothing interesting except another gun and a VHF radio.

'There's more to these men than we realise,' Waichari said uneasily. 'What's the transmitter for?' He stared hard at the gangsters who were hovering in the background, then at the car. 'Now I remember where I saw this car before. It was parked round a corner near your place on Saturday.'

'Was it?' Wekesa asked sharply.

Waichari turned his hard gaze on Wekesa. 'Yes. Were you expecting trouble on this trip? Was it the reason why you offered to accompany me?'

'I wasn't expecting this,' Wekesa replied. 'They must be gangsters who know I frequently make trips to Uganda with a lot of money. They were hanging around to observe the proper moment to rob me.'

Waichari thought this over and was not convinced, but he could think of no other explanation.

They removed the distributor cap of the black car with all its wires, punctured the other three tyres and wrecked the radio. After that they went to their own car and started the engine.

'Let me warn you,' Waichari told the gangsters

menacingly. 'You have got off very lightly. I don't know why you were tailing us, but if I catch you at it again, you had better have epitaphs ready for your tombstones.'

As they resumed their journey, they had a feeling they had made a couple of deadly enemies it would pay to watch out for.

'This safari is proving to be more eventful than I thought,' said Waichari. 'What do we do with these guns?'

'Keep them in a safe place. We might need them.'

A little further on they came across the lorry waiting for them, and they led it through more forest areas. As the sun rose they entered a highland area with maize, wheat and wattle trees. The traffic on the road was increasing.

'My goodness! Look!' Waichari said, pointing at two dark cars coming from the opposite direction. 'It is the police.'

'It's all right,' said Wekesa. Three heavy lorries, two trailers and a police jeep were following the two patrol cars. 'The police are escorting that convoy of coffee to the coast.'

'You mean our fine guardians of the law actually protect contraband goods?'

'I told you that some police chiefs are in it,' Wekesa replied. 'They get thirty per cent of the total sales. It is a staggering amount for a single convoy like this.'

Closer and closer came the convoy. Then it passed with a deafening roar. After the police jeep at the rear had passed, an orange Volvo appeared ahead.

'The owner of the convoy,' Wekesa explained. 'Look, it is one of the big fellows I was talking about.

You must have seen him many times on TV preaching about nation-building to the public, but he is more concerned with building his wealth.'

'How can such people expect to be convincing when they talk about fruits of independence while they grab so much for themselves?'

They travelled towards Kitale, past plain land with animals such as antelope, and then to another area where sisal and pineapples grew. They came across a junction and Wekesa turned right into cooler countryside with hills, maize, wheat and sunflowers. Soon a huge mountain loomed ahead. Waichari got tired of watching the scenery and dozed off.

Later, Wekesa patted his shoulder and Waichari opened his eyes. He saw that they had stopped in the main street of a trading centre, which was situated in the middle of a forest area. It was typical of numerous centres he had seen, but there were many people and vehicles of all types. The sun had climbed higher into the sky, and it looked as if it was going to be an excellent Monday.

'We've arrived,' said Wekesa. 'This is Chepkube, the infamous Black Gold City!'

# Chapter 5

Waichari was surprised by the so-called Black Gold City. 'It is just a nice, quiet little town,' he said. 'I think people exaggerate the details of it.'

Wekesa laughed. 'Wait until night comes, then you'll see.'

'What am I supposed to do now?'

'Find temporary lodgings, rest, and then search out a buyer for your property during the evening in the bars. He in turn will supply you with the black gold. I think I'll hang around for tonight and help you, and then resume my journey to Kampala in the morning.'

'I'd appreciate it,' said Waichari, wondering again why Wekesa was offering to do all this. He recalled the gangsters and decided there was definitely a catch, but Wekesa's help was welcome all the same.

They went to the residential houses behind the shops and Wekesa, who was well-known, found a landlord who rented them two small rooms. The price was high. Waichari and Wekesa occupied one of the rooms and Mutua and the turn-boys the other. After making the rooms habitable, they parked the vehicles at the front. Then they all went for a meal in a hotel, after which the crew was allowed to go and rest while Wekesa showed Waichari around.

The town was surrounded by forest. Here the coffee deals took place. There were often quarrels and fights over the deals. The few policemen and customs officials in town were lured into bars and kept busy drinking while the racket was going on.

On the outskirts of Chepkube there were slum-type shanties. They were mainly occupied by hawkers, house servants, charcoal dealers, destitutes and the jobless. The slum dwellers were often responsible for the pickpocketing incidents and night time robberies.

'You'll have to take care of your money or your work will be in vain,' Wekesa warned. 'Anyhow, you'll see for yourself what kind of place it is. For now, I suggest we return to our room and rest. Here, daytime is the time for rest; at night people become active.'

'Where do you think you're going, Waitherero?' Muna asked. They had just come home from school, changed and taken lunch. Muna had picked up a panga to go and feed the cattle, but Waitherero appeared to be going out, for she was walking towards the gate. She stopped at Muna's question.

'I am going to Janet's place,' she said. 'Why do you ask?'

'You should do something useful like cultivating those cabbages.'

'Why should I cultivate for Kanyi's wife?' she asked. 'How much longer do you expect us to stay here?'

'We should put some reliance on Waichari and do as he says,' Muna told her. 'We have no choice.'

Just then, Janet Waruguru came walking down to them from the road. She was cross.

'Hello' she said, in her quiet voice. 'People can hear you shouting from the road. What is the trouble?'

'Waichari instructed us to work on the farm as usual, Janet,' Muna explained. 'But Waitherero is refusing.'

'Why should you tire yourselves?'

'Then you, too, don't think much of our brother, do you?'

'I don't,' Janet said quietly but with much feeling.

Now even if Waitherero thought it was alright to let off steam against her brother Waichari, she didn't think it right for outsiders to speak ill of him, not even her friend Janet.

'Why have you been so hostile against my brother lately?' Waitherero asked. 'Is it because of this disgrace?'

'Partly, but something happened in my home on Friday for which I'll not forgive him. He doesn't know and I didn't tell him. Please don't ask me to tell you, because I'll not tell you either. I came to check on how you are and see if you have any problems.'

'We have none except for water shortage,' Waitherero replied. 'I was just coming to your place before you came. Now that you've come we might as well stay here. Come and help me sew and cook.'


In the forest area between Nakuru and Eldoret, a motorist in a red Peugeot 504 saloon car came across another car which appeared to have had a puncture.

The two unfortunate motorists with it had jacked the car up, but were looking at it helplessly. At the sight of the Peugeot, one of them waved beseechingly, and the Peugeot driver, a good samaritan, stopped his car.

'What is the problem, brothers?' he asked the unfortunate men, who were tall and black.

'Puncture. Help us with a wheel spanner, please.'

'I've got one, but you've got to hurry or I'll be late. You shouldn't travel without...' The Peugeot driver was about to open his car door to remove the spanner from the boot when he hesitated. There was something strange and tense about the men and there was something strange about their car. All the wheels were flat and a window was shattered.

The Peugeot driver engaged gear in a sudden panic, but it was too late. The big men had wrenched the doors open and got in. They seized the driver who struggled frantically as the car moved onward, out of control. The driver kept on kicking and lashing out furiously, but the two men were too strong for him. One of them had a short bar of steel, which he brought crashing down on the back of the driver's skull with savage force. The driver's world exploded into blackness with stars for the fraction of a second, then he knew no more. He collapsed just as the car was about to crash into the road bank. One of the attackers turned the steering-wheel sharply, but not before the car had scraped the road bank.

Taking control of the powerful car, one of the attackers, the stouter of the two, accelerated. When there was no other traffic in sight, they stopped the car and dragged the unconscious good samaritan into the forest. For a moment they glanced at his bleeding, fractured skull with emotionless faces, then left him for dead and returned to the car.

'What now, Yassim?' asked the driver, as they sped towards Eldoret at over a hundred miles an hour.

'We is gowin after them swines who ruined our car and robbed us, Abdalla,' the one called Yassim replied. 'And I is got a good idea where to find them.'


Back in his room in Chepkube, Waichari lay on his bed staring at the ceiling and wondering if he was going to be successful. He thought sadly of his sister, Janet, Kanyi and the gangsters and it was as if their hostility reached out to him.

Seeing darkness falling, he swung his legs on to the floor and slipped on his shoes. In a bed opposite, Wekesa was snoring, deep in sleep. Waichari shook him awake.

They both went to the shops, then Wekesa took Waichari around the few bars in town, looking for a suitable person to make a deal with.

The bars were crowded, and everyone was busy drinking, shouting, discussing business or dancing to the blare of deafening juke boxes. Wekesa seemed to be well-known and here and there someone shouted greetings. After going round two of the bars they went to the third, where a smart, thick-set *Mganda* was drinking beer.

'Hello, hello, Wekesa!' he said heartily. 'I haven't seen you for quite a while.'

They slapped hands in greeting. 'Meet Waichari, a business associate.'

'Pleased to meet you. Take a seat, boys, and join me in a drink.'

A woman brought beer for them and after a little small talk Wekesa said, 'I hate to butt in like this, but I have a little proposition that needs instant attention. Are you interested?'

'Let's have it.'

'Waichari here has a consignment of foodstuff for which he would like you to supply him with the black stuff in exchange.'

'What kind of black stuff?'

Waichari gave him a list. Ayub glanced at it, nodded, looked at it a little more carefully and frowned.

'It is too little. It doesn't justify the risk.'

This made Waichari uneasy, but Wekesa was unperturbed.

'Come now, Ayub, it is not all that contemptible. Besides, we have seven thousand in Kenyan currency. Are you taking the deal or do I find someone else?'

'What about transport?'

'We have a lorry.'

'And security?'

'We've guns and three able-bodied men.'

Ayub considered for a while, shrugged and said, 'Let's see the consignment.'

They finished the drinks, rose to their feet and walked out of the bar. They went to the lorry and found that the crew was ready. Wekesa suggested they look at the cargo in the forest, so they all climbed into the lorry and drove into the forest. There were lights and voices in the forest, where small-timers were carrying out transactions.

Mutua produced a flashlight, and Waichari, Wekesa and Ayub climbed into the rear of the lorry, while the crew stood outside at the back. Ayub inspected the cargo, then he and Wekesa started haggling over its equivalent in coffee sacks.

As they bargained, two pairs of hostile eyes watched the lorry from the edge of the forest. They belonged to tall, pitch dark men. One of them was heavier than the other.

'There be no doubt about it, Yassim,' the stout one said. 'It be the same lorry. Now we kill the pigs.'

Yassim sneered. 'How is you gowin to kill them? We is gowin to obey orders and return to report.'

Abdalla looked at his companion doubtfully. 'Be it wise to return? We have failed. It be wiser to kill the pigs and escape.'

'Where is we to escape? Not in Uganda, certainly. We get caught easily. We get caught in Kenya easily also for beating man and stealing car. No, we is gowin to report and bluff. Let we go in case the peejot fool recovers and gives alarm.'

They went to the forest where they had hidden the red Peugeot, got in and drove onward.

'We can't cross border with thieved car,' Yassim said. 'We is gowin to abandon it and cross on foot.'

They hid the car in a thicket, a kilometre from the border post and proceeded on foot. If Wekesa and Waichari had searched the duo's car well, they would have seen the diplomatic papers which they now showed at the border post, to enable them to cross.

On the Ugandan side of the border they waited for a private car to come by, showed the papers and demanded a lift, which the driver dare not refuse.

They went on their way into the Ugandan interior.

Not long afterwards, Waichari and company came along the same road. Waichari, Wekesa and Ayub, having reached a business agreement, were in the car. Mutua and one of the turn-boys followed in the lorry. They were to stop a little distance from the border for ten minutes; if anything went wrong, then the car would return and tell them to go back.

At the border there were three policemen, one of whom had a rifle, and a customs official.

'So it is you, is it?' the customs official growled. 'Where are you going this time and what are you carrying?'

'I am going to Kampala on business and the car is clean, sir,' said Wekesa.

'Is it?' the officer retorted. 'We shall see about that.'

As the officer went to open the boot of the car, Wekesa whispered to Waichari, 'Go and give him four hundred shillings. Say the car is clean and so is the lorry behind us.'

Waichari went to the rear of the car, and discreetly dropped the money into the boot as if by accident.

'The car is clean, sir, and so is the lorry which will be here shortly.'

The officer scowled at Waichari then nodded very slightly to the police, who waved the car on. The routine was repeated on the Ugandan side of the border, where there were three officers, and it cost him an extra three hundred Kenyan shillings. They drove on. When Mutua came to the border ten minutes later, he was waved on by the Kenyan and Ugandan officers. He saw the car waiting further on, and he followed it across a bridge, through a forest area with trading centres, and then along bush tracks. They were vigilant in case they came across soldiers. There could be no bribery with those. They would just spray the lorry with machine-gun fire and take everything they could carry. Those who survived the gunfire would be taken to the kangaroo court and then to the firing squad. However, they came to a town called Tororo without incident.

Here Ayub had a secret store where he kept coffee bought from farming estates and foodstuff from Kenya. Waichari gave Ayub the seven thousand he had in cash, and the tedious task of unloading the foodstuff began. According to their negotiations, Waichari would get eighty sacks of coffee. It was not exactly the number he had expected, but if Wekesa was to be believed, they would raise a small fortune. Loading them would be another tedious job and, even if Ayub supplied two men to help with the work, it would be a few hours before it was managed. Waichari wanted to recross the border before dawn, for he was working against time.

Yassim and Abdalla walked along the corridor of a grim, three-storey building, their stony faces frightened for once. At the rear of the building they stopped before an office, hesitated and then Yassim knocked at the door.

'Come in,' a gruff voice said.

The two tall men entered the office where a grim, well-fed officer sat studying a file. He was called Major Mulindwa, but he was better known as 'the Butcher'.

The duo saluted. Major Mulindwa glanced at them

and then went on studying the file while the two stood waiting silently, trembling. Finally, the Major wrote some notes in the file, closed it and frowned at them. 'It is high time I had a report from you two.'

'We followed the quarry from Nairobi as we radioed,' said Yassim, and went on to relate how Waichari and Wekesa ambushed them, robbed them and damaged the car. He went so far as to confess how they had had no choice but to hijack another car.

The major glanced at them in silent wrath. Then he produced a pistol with silencer from his desk, and the two rolled their eyes in fright.

'Mercy!' screamed Abdalla.

The major was furious. 'I give you two a job which a Sunday-school drop-out could handle, and you bungle it! Your lives are forfeited!'

So saying, the Butcher squeezed the trigger twice, making the gun spit lead with a muffled sound. The horrified victims shrieked, clutched at their stomachs, and collapsed on the floor.

The major returned the gun to its drawer, picked up a telephone and called four soldiers. 'I believe there is a tipper lorry outside for litter such as this,' he told them when they appeared, gesturing to the two dead men. 'And Sergeant, send someone with a bucket to clean up.'

The soldiers dragged the bodies out of the office, along the corridors and out of the main door. Sure enough, there was a tipper outside, whose blood-spattered interior contained four, smashed corpses in rags. Yassim and Abdalla's corpses were heaved aboard also.

After the bloodstains had been rinsed from the

floor of the major's office and the cleaner had departed, the mad major dialled a number. When his call was answered, he explained about the information the dead men had brought and how he had destroyed them.

'What do I do now, Chief?' he concluded by asking.

'Choose a more efficient couple of men and await instructions,' said the voice at the other end.

# Chapter 6

'Is this the kind of luck going to last?' Waichari asked himself next morning, as Mutua heaved a sack of coffee onto his back from the lorry. The lorry was parked at the back of a coffee store in Chepkube. He carried the sack into the store and dumped it inside. It was tedious work and he felt he would drop any minute. They had done too much loading and unloading that night.

Waichari looked at the others as they staggered in with their sacks. They were in no better shape. The unloading of foodstuff and loading of coffee in Tororo had gone on until four in the morning. They had crossed the border just before daylight, then they had gone back to look for a coffee dealer who would buy their coffee and see it to the coast. There were many African, Asian and Arab dealers in Chepkube, and Wekesa had recommended Kanji Shah, a small but shrewd Indian with whom he had dealt before. Kanji Shah, however, had refused to come up to Wekesa's expectations. Wekesa had asked for two thousand per bag, but Kanji Shah had only agreed to pay five hundred less. Even if Wekesa was far from satisfied, Waichari was happy enough, for it was still thrice the buying price. He considered the first trip to have been a success. Three or four more and he was going to beat the auction bell.

To minimise the risk he would have to make as few trips as possible, but make them as profitable as possible. Anyhow, the first trip had proved it was practically impossible to make a trip every day, especially if they were to deal in foodstuff as well. Daylight had nearly caught them in Uganda, and that was risky. If effective profits were to be expected from each trip, the lorry would be crossing the border filled with foodstuff and returning loaded with coffee. To minimise the risk even more, Waichari would have to have every route the lorry took scouted.

When the tedious job of unloading was finally ended, they drove the vehicles to their rooms behind the shops and then went to a hotel where they took a late breakfast.

'Not a bad beginning,' Waichari told his men. 'Take a rest, but in the afternoon we're going into the interior to buy foodstuff. We'll cross the border tomorrow evening.'

Later, after they had rested a little, Wekesa declared it was time for him to move on.

'Sorry, but my affairs in Uganda cannot wait.' Wekesa paused before continuing, 'However, if you'll accompany me to Kampala and let me hold consultations with my boss, we'll see if he can spare me for a little while. After all, you wanted to meet Njogu as well.'

It was true that Waichari wanted to meet Njogu, and he also needed Wekesa and his car, but he hesitated. It was obvious that Wekesa wanted to go to Kampala with Waichari. Why? What or who was Wekesa afraid of? Waichari recalled the gunmen who had followed them from Nairobi. However, being of a reckless nature, he gave his consent.

Leaving Mutua with money and instructions to buy the foodstuff in the nearest major town, he drove off with Wekesa in the car. Waichari was expecting trouble of some kind, but they crossed the border and sped past Tororo, Jinja and Lugazi without incident. Then they entered Kampala, the city built on seven hills. They stopped in front of a large store in a back street. They went into the office where the owner, an influential businessman called Sowedi, gave them a hearty welcome.

Mr Sowedi was a slim, cheerful looking man of fifty with lean features and streaks of white in his hair. He was wearing a dark suit and thin-rimmed glasses. He was Njogu's close friend and main business associate in Uganda. Mr Sowedi was influential in that his transactions with Njogu were carried out with apparent immunity from the ruthless Ugandan security forces, even when the country was at its most chaotic.

'Good afternoon, Mr Sowedi,' Wekesa said. 'This is Mr Mathu, a friend of mine who has come to do business, and he kindly offered to escort me.'

'Delighted to meet you, Mr Mathu,' Sowedi said, turning his beaming face on Waichari and giving him a hearty handshake also. 'Any friend of Njogu's and Wekesa's is my friend, too.'

Sowedi kept talking until he learned of the circumstances which had brought them to Uganda. 'Things have got out of hand in Nairobi, and I wanted to consult the boss,' Wekesa explained. 'Since I expected him to be with you, I rang you twice a few days ago, but you were not in. Your secretary informed me that he had left, but she did not tell me where he had gone. Since I have urgent matters to discuss with him, I could not wait for him to return to Kenya, so I decided to come personally. I believe he informed you where he went, sir.'

'Yes, he is in Rwanda where I found him a contract to transport Rwandese coffee to Mombasa. Some of my vehicles are with him. It will be quite an impressive convoy. I am expecting him next Tuesday in the morning.

'How can I contact him?'

'Through the Coffee Marketing Board. I have the phone number somewhere.' Sowedi pulled out a drawer, rummaged in it and then changed his mind. 'Can't the matters wait? He instructed me that he should only be consulted in matters of dire emergency.' Sowedi rummaged in the drawer again and produced a note. Wekesa glance at it. It was typed and brief. It simply said: Gone to Rwanda for business and rest. Be back on Tuesday 19. I'll deal with any problems then.

Njogu had signed it at the bottom. Sowedi took the letter back. 'It was for anyone who wanted him. Why don't you come here on Tuesday at ten and accompany him to the coast?'

'I will,' Wekesa said, disappointed, 'since I have no choice but to wait.' Wekesa rose to his feet. 'Thanks very much for your time. Since I want to keep clear of Nairobi headaches, I'll hang around western Kenya with my friend here until Njogu returns. Be seeing you on Tuesday.'

'Be looking forward to seeing you,' Sowedi replied, studying Waichari as the latter rose to his feet in his slow manner, putting on his hat. 'I'll also look forward to furthering your acquaintance, Mr Mathu.

Perhaps we could do business?'

'Thanks, but I don't think I am in your league. I am only a small timer.'

They left the jolly Kampula magnate. Waichari liked him. Immediately afterwards, they drove to a petrol station, where Wekesa talked with the service man in a low voice as he filled the car. Then, after eating at a hotel, the duo drove back to Chepkube.

Just as Waichari had feared, the second trip was not so good. It began with the officials on the Ugandan side of the border refusing to take bribes, and threatening to seize both the truck and the crew if they ventured across. It appeared that they were either afraid, or they had taken too many bribes that day and had to look for a scapegoat to show that they were on duty. But Waichari could not afford to be a scapegoat or to turn back. He and Wekesa came out of the car to plead with the officials while the lorry hovered at a discreet distance on the Kenyan side of the border.

After a long argument, Waichari bribed his way through with three thousand shillings, a sum he could ill afford. As they went on into the interior, with Waichari and Wekesa ever-vigilant in the car, rain began to fall. It made the going extemely difficult since they were using bush tracks. The lorry stuck in the mud twice, but they dared not stop until daylight. It would have been suicide. They lay branches on the track to enable the lorry to move on. The only consolation to be derived from the weather was that it was unlikely that the security forces were abroad. They arrived at Ayub's store in

Tororo at around midnight, tired, wet and muddy. This resulted in their being late on their return trip, and being caught by daylight. They were spotted by a couple of policeman, and it was indeed lucky for them that the policemen took bribes, or that would have been the end of Waichari's new career. At the border he had to bribe his way through again.

'This bribery business will finish me!' Waichari complained.

'It's all part of the racket,' Wekesa said. 'I told you, you have to keep a certain percentage aside for protection.'

After the sale of the second consignment of a hundred and two sacks, Waichari discovered that he had made a slight financial improvement, but it was not good enough because of the heavy expenses. He had to make the next two trips as effective as possible, hoping that nothing would go wrong.

Waichari and his confederates spent Friday resting and buying foodstuff in Bungoma, while Ayub looked for coffee in eastern Ugandan states. In the evening they crossed the border. The heavily laden truck moved slowly while the car moved ahead, scouting every route. The roads were in a better condition, but what Waichari had been fearing all the time happened; they ran into soldiers.

They had parked a Land-Rover at a small trading centre and, judging from the noise and screams that came from the surrounding houses, they were on the rampage, beating, robbing and raping the villagers. Only one of the soldiers was guarding the Land-Rover. No sooner did Wekesa sight the Land-Rover in his headlights than he turned the car the way it had come.

'Hey! Stop or I shoot!' yelled the soldier, drawing a pistol. As Wekesa accelerated, the pistol spat lead and fire, but the car was out of range of the small firearm. As it vanished at high speed, the soldier leapt into the driving seat of the Land-Rover and sounded the horn urgently. One by one half a dozen soldiers in battle uniform, carrying sub-machine guns, came hurrying from the village. The soldier hurriedly explained to his sergeant what had happened.

'After them!' yelled the sergeant. 'Mow the crooks down and then burn them!' They all scrambled into the Land-Rover and it roared off after the car.

Over a mile ahead, Waichari was urging Wekesa to drive faster. 'We mustn't be caught!' he yelled.

'We can get away, but the lorry can't!' Wekesa said fearfully. 'We'll get your men into the car and escape, and let them do what they like with the lorry.'

'Never! I'd rather die. I am going to fight.'

'Die you mean! You will if you fight, and they will still get the lorry anyway. We had better think of something else, quickly.'

Waichari saw the sense of this, and thought desperately as the car roared across the bush country at high speed. It left the pursuing Land-Rover further behind. Presently they came across the lorry which was lumbering onwards with dimmed lights, its body shuddering under the weight of its load. As the car stopped abreast the lorry, Waichari jumped out and yelled to Mutua urgently, 'Soldiers! Put out the lights, drive into the bush and cut the engine! Hide and then proceed to destination if we succeed in getting them away!'

Panic stricken, Mutua hastily switched off the lights and swerved the metal monster off the road, driving it blindly sixty metres into the bush before it scraped against a tree and came to a halt. Mutua turned the engine off.

'Move over, I'll drive,' said Waichari harshly, getting into the car.

'What's the idea?' Wekesa asked, moving to the passenger seat while Waichari slid under the driving wheel.

'We'll act as a decoy and hope Mutua will get away while they pursue us. But they may have seen the lorry lights or heard the engine sound. Shoot at them to make sure they are more interested in us!'

Wekesa cocked his gun and as Waichari drove the car onward, the Land-Rover appeared round a bend. Wekesa fired rapidly three times.

'Whaat?' the sergeant yelled in disbelief. 'They're armed! They are rebels! They must have stopped to warn their friends whose lights we saw. But where is that other car? It must be ahead! After them!'

The sergeant's words were drowned out by the roar of machine-gun fire. Even if the car was out of range, the bullets were too close for Waichari's comfort, and in his fright he drove the car faster and faster, punishing the engine to the maximum.

The chase went on and on, and since the soldiers' vehicle was built more for power and endurance than for speed, they were gradually left behind. Waichari branched off twice, then drove with parking lights for half an hour. When he was sure they had lost the soldiers, he drove into the bushes as Mutua had done and cut off the engine.

Waichari sighed and said, 'This business is

getting dirtier and dirtier. I hope that is the last we see of them. I hope Mutua had the nerve to drive on as soon as the course was clear as I instructed him.'

'He might make it. But we might run into trouble if we try to make it across the border tonight.'

'I can't really afford to lose a single day, but I guess I have little choice in the matter.'

Waichari got out of the vehicle and surveyed the countryside. He could see the lights of the Land-Rover as it wandered afar. He wondered what Janet would say if she saw him now, being hunted like a wild beast or a criminal. Come to think of it, he was a criminal. How low he had stooped! 'If you can't take care of your own affairs, how can you take care of someone else?' Why did the taunt keep haunting him?

The lights of the Land-Rover gleamed farther and farther away until finally they disappeared.

'Do you think they will be back?' Wekesa, who had also got out of the car, asked.

'I don't think so, but let's get going in case they do.'

When they finally reached Ayub's store, they were relieved to find Mutua had made it, but he complained that the racket was proving to be too dangerous for his liking, since he had a family back home. The rest of the night was taken up with unloading the food-stuff, and they spent the next day resting and looking for six armed contraband-ists who would guard the lorry up to the border. Waichari could not risk his cargo being seized. It was his biggest consignment so far; a hundred and twenty sacks which filled the lorry.

At midnight they made for the border, more

vigilant then ever, but they crossed without incident. The trouble was that there was still a considerable amount of money to be raised and, after the episode of the soldiers, Waichari, like his crew, was beginning to lose his nerve.

# Chapter 7

Next morning found Waichari, Wekesa and Mutua resting on the grass in front of their room at Chepkube. The turn-boys were guarding the lorry nearby. Waichari was worried because Kanji Shah had closed his shop. It was a Sunday. This meant there would be no unloading of the coffee they had brought during the night until the next day. The prospect of a full day of inactivity alarmed Waichari, since time was running out for him. Mutua was probably brooding over the unnerving prospect of crossing the border again, and was likely to cause trouble when the time came. It was hard to guess what was troubling Wekesa, since he did not voice his thoughts, but he seemed as worried as the other two.

Waichari rose to his feet and started pacing about restlessly. 'I think I'll take a walk to clear my head,' he said.

'I'll join you,' Wekesa said, sitting up and tying his shoelaces.

Waichari turned to the brooding Mutua. 'You need a bit of cheering also. Would you like to join us?'

'No, I'll stay here and rest.'

Waichari and Wekesa left and walked along behind the shops. Idly they began to comment on all the girls they passed. 'Too artificial,' Waichari remarked about one, and they passed her by. 'Too old,' he remarked about another.

'There are four more over there plaiting their hair,' Wekesa said, pointing.

'Let's go and inspect. I'll be the judge, for I have a diploma in that sort of judgement.'

Grinning wickedly, Wekesa followed the tall and slow moving Waichari to the girls, who were plaiting their hair under a tree. They stopped near them, and the women turned to look at them. Waichari studied them. 'The brown one looks promising,' he said playfully.

'Yes,' Wekesa agreed with enthusiasm. 'She would be okay for me. How do we get her away from the rest?'

'With this type you only have to snap your fingers.'

Waichari walked up to the seated women in his slow manner, a smile on his face. They observed his advance with curiosity.

'How are you, sisters?' he greeted them in Kiswahili, lifting his hat.

'We are fine,' they answered, eyeing him curiously.

Waichari smiled disarmingly, then looked straight at the brown beauty. 'Actually, it's you I wanted to see. I have a message for you from a friend.'

'Who?'

'I'll tell you if you let me see you for a moment.'

'Where is this person who sent you, and who are you?'

'He is nearby, and as for my identity, I am called the bearer of good tidings,' Waichari replied. 'There is no harm in listening, is there? Come aside and I'll tell you.' He held out a hand to help her up.

Wekesa was delighted to see the brown beauty rise to her feet, straighten her slippery blue dress and follow Waichari to where he was standing.

'What is this message you are talking about?' the girl asked impatiently.

Waichari ignored the question and said, 'I am Mathu and this is my pal Wekesa. He is overwhelmed with desire to talk to you.'

'I don't know him,' she said.

'In Kikuyland, where I come from,' Waichari told her, 'there is a saying that to talk to one another is to love one another. So I want you to talk to one another very, very gently, and we'll see if you won't cope.'

Wekesa and the girl talked for five minutes and seemed to come to an agreement.

The girl, who called herself Helena, followed them and Waichari began to look for a companion. Just then, he noticed a girl moving away from the town. There was something about her which caught his interest. 'She will do,' he declared and hurried across the street after her.

As he caught up with the girl, he said, 'Ah, there you are,' as if she was a long lost friend. 'I've found you at last!'

She stopped, studied him and looked puzzled. 'Who are you?'

'Allow me to introduce myself. I am Mathu. Can you, without taking offence, tell me your name?'

'It is Nanjala.'

'It is good of you to tell me,' Waichari told her, and as he shook her hand he realised why she had caught his interest. She was the same size as Janet, and had the same kind of healthy figure and skin. But this one was a little younger and darker, and she had short hair.

'Well, Nanjala, I would regret losing this chance of getting to know you. Why don't you accompany me back to town and let us get better acquainted?'

'Another time. I am going home to wash my clothes.'

'I really feel we should be friends. Come on, sister, let me buy you a soda and let's have a chat. I promise you won't regret it.'

'I don't think I should.'

As she stood hesitating, Waichari took her hand and gently but firmly led her back towards the shops. Her resistance was half-hearted. At the shops, the couple were joined by Wekesa and his girl, and Waichari ordered a round of sodas. While they sipped, Nanjala agreed to go for a walk with Waichari in the countryside, while Wekesa was to be taken to Helena's place to play records and take drinks. After the sodas were finished, Waichari took Nanjala's hand.

'See you later, Wekesa. Have a good time.'


Major Mulindwa, sitting in his office behind his desk, listened intently to the telephone.

'Right, chief,' he said gruffly. He pressed off the call and dialled another.

'Hello, this is the SSS 009,' answered the voice at the other end. The SSS 009 was one of a number of secret murder squads that Amin used to stay in power.

'This is Major Mulindwa of the State Research

Bureau. Put me through to your chief.'

After a while, another voice came on the line.

'Hello, Major, what can I do for you?'

'You promised me a couple of operatives. I need them now, and make sure that they are most efficient. This is important.'

'All right, I'll see what I can do.'

The line went dead and Major Mulindwa put the phone down. He picked up a fresh file and started scribbling notes. He was still doing so ten minutes later when there was a knock at the door.

'Come in.'

Two Arabs in plain clothes entered. One of them was middle-aged, scarred and fierce looking. The other was young and handsome. The older one gave a reluctant salute.

'We have been instructed by the SSS 009 chief to report to you, Major.'

'Ah, yes, please sit down.'

The Arabs sat down and waited. The major closed his file, leaned back in his chair and studied them. He concluded they were not the type to have a misunderstanding with. 'We are interested in a couple of Kenyan contrabandists,' he began. 'You know we are losing millions through the coffee smuggling racket at the border. We lose valuable foreign exchange to Kenya when her racketeers sell our coffee for us. They are thorns in our flesh. Our attention had been drawn to one of them, who has caused much damage to our economy, and he must be dealt with accordingly. He has a companion or two. I have their descriptions here.' The major patted the file he had been writing in. 'Do you follow me?'

The Arabs nodded.

'Excellent,' said the major. 'This is what you are going to do...'

Meanwhile, Waichari and Nanjala had crossed the river and were walking through a village near Chepkube. By now he had put her at ease and she was chatting freely with him. She was bold, lively and talkative, unlike the quiet Janet.

The local people they came across lived in thatched houses, and didn't appear to be much influenced by foreign culture.

'From which tribe are they?' Waichari asked.

'They are my people, the Babukusu,' said Nanjala.

'How do they spend their leisure time?'

'Feasting and traditional dances are frequent. They also drink maize beer called *kwete.*'

They came across some villagers who were feasting on goat meat and beer. 'It is one of the parties I described,' said Nanjala, delighted. 'They must be celebrating a birth or something. Let us join them.'

'Then you know the host?'

'All are welcome to this kind of party.'

'Ah, African hospitality as I like it!' Waichari said approvingly, and followed her to the merrymakers.

There were over a dozen people of all ages. Among them were three musicians. Nanjala got Waichari a mug of beer and a plate of meat, and he soon felt at home.

Suddenly a drum started booming rhythmically, then a ring of steel was rung and a horn was blown. The three musicians started singing but their voices were lost in the din their instruments were making.

As the beat caught heat, one by one people started jumping here and there to the rhythm. Soon everyone, young and old, joined the dance. Even Nanjala did. Waichari got carried away as well and went to the middle of the dancers. He hopped and skipped around, making people laugh. On and on went the cacophony while people jumped around in unison. Now and then someone yelled or blew through his mouth in enjoyment. After the dance the happy party-crashing couple went on with their walk.

Waichari put his arm round Nanjala's waist and steered her towards a bush track.

'There are no dwellings that way. Only bush country.'

'I want to look at the countryside. Aren't you an admirer of natural beauty?'

Nanjala stretched her arm towards the bushes, forests and huge mountain ahead of them. 'I have seen all this all my life and I don't see much in it. I would prefer cities with tall buildings, fine cars and gay lights.'

Waichari sat down and gestured to her to do the same.

'I want to rest a bit,' he said, and she sat beside him.

'You should be grateful to live in such an unspoiled environment,' he continued. 'Doesn't it feel nice to rest on green grass like this, with a cool breeze blowing in your face instead of dust and fumes, and the sounds the singing birds instead of heavy diesel engines?'

Nanjala giggled, swinging her legs, 'You're funny. You sound almost like my biology teacher.'

Waichari grinned down at her. 'Relax. I am not

such a serious student of nature, but only talking...'

'Hush. I believe I hear voices,' Nanjala interrupted him.

Waichari strained his ears. 'I don't hear any – Wait! Now I do. They are getting louder and louder. Sounds as if a quarrel is brewing.'

Soon they didn't have to strain to hear the voices of several angry men, over two hundred metres away. They rose to their feet and hurried through the bushes.

As they got closer to the men, their voices rose higher and higher with rage. Soon the couple came to a clearing where two groups of peasants were playing tug-of-war with heavy sacks. Everyone was yelling at the top of their voices in a dialect Waichari could not understand.

'I wonder what is going on,' he said, as they watched from the edge of the clearing.

Nanjala listened and, clinging to his arm, she explained. 'They are quarrelling over those sacks of coffee which have been smuggled across the border. Each of the groups wants to buy the coffee, but neither will give in to the other.'

The leader of one group, a big man in a white shirt and khaki shorts, suddenly let go of a sack. He sent his fist crashing into the face of one of the rival group, and the man went sprawling on to the grass. His friends abandoned the sacks also and leaped at the big man's men, and the battle was truly joined. What was terrible about the fight was that both sides were armed with knives and clubs, and one man had a hammer. It was a fierce fight, totally devoid of fairness or mercy.

The big man's group was winning because he was strong. Unfortunately for him, one of his adversaries was the man who had the hammer. While the big man was booting a fallen victim, he came up on the big man from behind and hit him on the back of the head with the hammer. The big man pitched forward and fell on the grass, his nose and the back of his head turning crimson with blood. As the hammer came down with savage force, Nanjala let out a piercing shriek. Waichari shifted at last as he realised that he was not watching a movie but stark reality. He put his arm around the hysterical girl and steered her away from the scene.

'Murder!' he breathed, feeling sick. 'What a monster! Is life worth a sack of coffee? Trust men to ruin a beautiful environment with their evil! Let's get as far away from here as possible. I don't want to be involved.'

Nanjala did not reply, but kept whimpering in her hysteria, following him blindly.

They made their way back to the town and Waichari bought brandy to steady their nerves, and ordered a small meal to be specially made. By the time the meal was ready and they had finished the bottle, it was late, and Nanjala was feeling better. It was time to take her to his room, but he hesitated. Haunting him constantly was the vision of another girl back home.

'Am I turning soft?' he asked himself.

As he took Nanjala's hand and led her out of the hotel room where they had been dining, Janet remained with him in his mind, making him inwardly ashamed.

When he unlocked the door of his room and

invited Nanjala in, Mutua called from the next room.

'Waichari, Wekesa told me to inform you he is spending the night elsewhere.'

Waichari could guess where. 'You must not mind the scant furniture,' he told Nanjala. 'This is only a temporary lodging.'

'Where do you come from?' she asked.

'From Central Province.'

'Did you come to do *magendo*?'

'I suppose it is futile for me to deny it.'

'I feel you can do more important things. Why did you choose *magendo*?'

'Because of circumstances, my dear,' he answered her vaguely, gathering her into his arms. He hugged her until, gradually, he felt her comfortable body breathe faster, quiver and yield to his own.

# Chapter 8

Wekesa seemed to have been cheered by the night of love making as they took breakfast next morning, but Waichari had not.

'What's the matter with you?' Wekesa asked him.

'I guess I didn't have enough sleep,' Waichari lied.

The truth of the matter was that he was feeling a little ashamed of himself and unclean, and he didn't have to search his mind to know what had brought about the change in him. It was Janet Waruguru who was pricking his conscience. He had tried to tell himself that since she had no use for him, it didn't matter what he did with other girls, but her memory kept nagging at him and making him feel guilty all the same.

'What's the schedule for the day?' Wekesa asked.

'We'll sell and unload the last consignment of coffee and then go to Kitale for more foodstuff. We ought to be back by evening.'

'Don't forget that tomorrow is Tuesday, when we go to Kampala to meet Njogu. Sowedi informed us he is returning then, remember?'

'I haven't forgotton,' Waichari informed him. 'As a matter of fact I am looking forward to meeting the big shot to see if I can borrow a little capital from him. It would save me these nightmare crossings. But whether he'll help me or not, we'll have to be back here in Chepkube by evening to take the food across the border.'

'How many more trips do you need to raise the required sum?'

'Two more, if we're lucky.'

Mutua, however, didn't think their luck would hold, and he informed Waichari so in no uncertain terms. As they walked from the back of the hotel to the lorry, the driver fell in step with Waichari. After a little hesitation, Mutua began, 'We've made three trips across the border. We are unscathed so far, but such luck can't last. Venturing across the border again would be driving our luck too far. I suggest we stop while the going is good.'

Waichari had been half expecting this. He stopped and stood studying the well-built driver.

'Look here, Mutua. You know I don't like this racket any more than you do. You know what drove me to it. I have still got a considerable sum to raise and I can't quit now because I have no alternative. Or have you got any other idea?'

'No, but isn't it better to lose one's property than to lose one's life?'

'I have asked myself the same question, Mutua, and I have concluded I'd rather risk my life. It is more than a question of saving my heritage, it is my honour as well. I am going to quit the racket after raising what I need, but not before. I didn't force you to come with me, and I am not going to force you to go on. Are you going to go on helping me or do I have to find another driver?'

Mutua was uncomfortable. 'You may be the boss, but I am older and I have seen much. I didn't like what I saw in Uganda, and I dislike what we might find there in future even more. I suggest you think twice before going there to do *magendo* again. I say this not as one who wishes you well. You must not think I can desert you but I am afraid for myself, for you and for all of us.'

Without waiting to hear Waichari's reply, Mutua moved onward. Waichari stood looking after him. The trusted driver's last words had made him more uneasy.

For the next five hours he had no time to think, because everyone was busy unloading the large consignment of coffee they had brought on Saturday night from the lorry and carrying it into Kanji Shah's store. The problem troubled him all the same. What troubled him even more was his behaviour the night before, and he had an urge to know where Janet was and what she was doing. He also wanted to know how things were at home and to try to reassure his emotional sister.

After the unloading and transactions were over, Waichari asked Kanji Shah to let him use his phone. He booked a call to his store in his home area, and it was an hour before it went through.

'Hello. This is Mathu Wholesale Store,' said a bored voice at the other end.

'Hello, Father of Kambo. This is Waichari speaking. How are things going?'

'I've still got a little stock left, worth about two thousand, two hundred shillings.'

'I see. How much have you got in cash?'

'Two thousand, four hundred. I am hoping it will have reached four thousand by the time you get back.'

'Excellent work, Father of Kambo!' Waichari said

with sincere gratitude. 'I want to talk to my sister. See if you can find her at school before she goes home for lunch.'

'I shall. Hang on.'

Waichari waited, feeling pleased with the old man. He wished he could be successful in his enterprising also, and have this terrible burden of the loan behind him. So far things had not gone too badly. If only his luck held, despite Mutua's warning!

Ten minutes later, his young sister's little voice came on the line. She was panting as if she had been running. 'Hello, Waichari. Is it really you?'

'Yes, it is.'

'How are you? Are you all right?' There was a genuine concern in her voice. Despite her hostility he knew she was a kind and loving sister at heart.

'Yes. How are you yourself? You need not tell me. If I know you, you've been worrying yourself sick, hardly listening to what your teachers are saying. Isn't that so, Waitherero?'

There was a pause, then she admitted it was so. 'Thanks to you,' she added unkindly.

'How many times must I tell you to leave the worrying to me, Waitherero?'

'When are you coming back?'

'On Thursday, if everything goes according to plan. Now give me news from your end. How are things at home?'

'As you left them, but there has been an acute shortage of water, and Kanyi has been with friends to view the farm again.'

'I thought I advised that fat fraud to keep clear of our property,' Waichari breathed in fury. 'He is asking for trouble. Ignore him. I hope Muna has not starved the cattle and you've not neglected the gardens?'

'We are feeding the cattle, but I shan't cultivate the farm for Kanyi.'

'You really must learn to respect my wishes.' Then he asked the question which had prompted him to make the call. 'How is your friend Waruguru?'

'I don't know.'

Waichari was surprised. 'What do you mean, you don't know?'

'I haven't seen her for days. She hasn't been here to see me and since I felt she had let me down I haven't been to her home to see her, either. Last time she was here, she talked of going to Nyeri for a secretarial course. I think she has left already.'

Waichari gripped the receiver hard, feeling sick with disappointment. The one person he would have counted on in their hour of need had deserted them. This was terrible! Waichari stood not knowing what to say or think. All he knew was that the world would never be the same for him again.

'Hello! Are you still there?' Waitherero asked.

'Yes.'

As if she sensed his disappointment, she went on, 'I believe she sincerely wishes you the best of luck.'

'Good of her,' Waichari commented without much cheer.

'But I don't know what you've done to her to...' Waitherero hesitated, then continued, 'I mean you've wronged her and she won't forgive you. She didn't tell me how, but it was something to do with her home. I think that is why she has gone away.'

'Wronged her? In what way? I don't remember

abusing her or her family in any way!'

'You have, apparently. Think how, for it is you who drove her away from me.'

Waichari paused, then said, 'Thanks for the information, sister. Goodbye till I return.'

'Goodbye and good luck, Waichari.'

Waichari put the phone down, thanked the Indian and left the store in a depressed state. He walked to the edge of the forest in his slow manner, removed his shoes and lay face down on the green grass. He wanted to collect his thoughts.

'So she is gone,' he said to himself. 'Well, I had been expecting it, but not so soon. What can I have done to wrong her? Surely the debt does not justify the kind of hostility she has shown me.'

Oh, well, he had no choice but to let her go. After all, he did not want a woman who was ready to believe the worst of him. And yet, hadn't Janet given him a chance to explain how he had got into disgrace, and he had failed to do so to protect his father's name? She was only human, and could do nothing but blame him. So he would let her go without any ill-feeling. It was a pity, though. She would have taken care of the farm and home as his mother had done, while he took care of the business. But it was no use thinking of this.

Waichari's mind shifted to Kanyi, who was tormenting his family. To frustrate Kanyi, he had to clear the loan, and to clear it he had to make another trip which Mutua warned would be dangerous.

He respected Mutua's views, but he had to go ahead and make the trip. It would have to be the biggest trip of all, with the lorry overloaded. Perhaps Wekesa would find him a better market for the stuff, then all his financial troubles would be over. But if he made the slightest mistake, then everything would be lost. Waichari lay thinking carefully, planning the trip.

Meanwhile, in the old three-storey building in Kampala, a soldier was hurrying through the corridors. He went round a corner to the office of Major Mulindwa, the Butcher. But the major was not in. The soldier hurried to the cells. He knocked at the first door and it was opened. A prisoner was being interrogated by a group of officers, and what was being done to him is best left unprinted. Here he was directed to the whereabouts of the major.

The soldier heard his gruff voice in the next cell. He knocked at the door and the major told him to come in. Even the toughened soldier shuddered at the sight of the major. The latter, who was guarded by two more soldiers, was holding a knife in one hand, a piece of human tissue in the other which he had cut from the thigh of an unconscious man on the floor.

The victim was wearing a tattered, bloody, dark suit, and his body was mutilated with knife cuts. Watching in fascinated horror were a dozen more prisoners, who were bruised from beatings and thin from starvation.

The soldier saluted. 'Message on the radio for you, sir.'

'Excellent,' said the Butcher. He made to depart, but paused in the doorway to address the dozen prisoners. 'I fear time is running out for you parasites, but I am going to make the most of it.'

The soldiers with the major locked the door while he hurried to the radio, where he proceeded to receive a brief report from the Arabs. After that the major returned to his office and rang the chief.

'Every post has been alerted, sir, and the SSS 009 operatives are in position,' the major reported. 'The Kenyan contrabandists will not escape.'

'Excellent, excellent,' said the chief. 'If preparations are complete, then we can go ahead and prepare for bloodbath and holocaust.'

# Chapter 9

Waichari bathed and then put on a grey suit with long sleeves. They were going to meet the big shot Njogu in Kampala, as Mr Sowedi had suggested. They had returned to Chepkube from Kitale last night in the car. They had left the lorry and its crew in Kitale where they had bought their next cargo. Since there had been so much loading to do, night had fallen without their being able to complete it all, so Waichari had instructed the crew to go on loading the goods today, while he and Wekesa went to Kampala. They were all to meet in Chepkube later that evening, ready for the last crossing.

After breakfast the two men went to Wekesa's car and then they were on their way. The sun was warming up and it looked as if it was going to be a fine day.

Waichari was driving while Wekesa sat relaxed in the passenger seat. They had formed a habit of taking turns at the wheel. Presently they pulled up at the border point. By now Waichari was familiar to the officials on both sides of the border. On the Kenya side they were allowed to cross without any problem, but on the Uganda side they were scrutinised by three policemen who knew them, but who looked at them as if they had never seen them before.

'Is there anything wrong?' Wekesa asked them anxiously. 'I assure you that my associate here is having his papers processed.'

'Everything is okay,' the sergeant in charge told them, and waved them on.

No sooner was the car out of sight than the sergeant rushed to a telephone and rang a certain number in Kampala.

'This is Lwakhakha border point,' the sergeant said when he was through. 'The contrabandist you alerted us to watch out for has just passed through. He is with a fellow-smuggler. They are in a Ford Escort KQF 325.'

'Good work,' said a gruff voice at the other end. 'Just make sure they are not allowed to go back.'

In an office in Nakasero, Kampala, the Butcher pressed off the call and dialled another, which went through almost instantly.

'They've been sighted, chief!' the Butcher said with excitement.

'I knew it!' the voice at the other end replied with equal excitement. 'I am coming over for the final arrangements. In the meantime, Major, you know what to do.'

The Butcher put the phone down, left the office and hurried through the corridors. He went to the receiver which had been tuned to a certain frequency, ready for transmission.

'FXY calling SSS,' he said into the microphone.

'Are you reading me?'

'Roger,' the speaker responded.

'Quarry has been sighted at Lwakhakha post *en route* to Kampala. Do as you were instructed and then report with all possible speed. Is that clear?'

'Roger.'

'You must not fail, for we have no use for failures.
Over and out.'

On a country road in eastern Uganda, in a blue
car with an antenna, the two Arabic operatives from
the SSS 009 turned from the radio and looked at
each other. The older, fierce-looking one put the
microphone down and nodded to the younger one.
The young one started the engine and drove off at
high speed.

After passing several trading centres in the forest
area, Waichari and Wekesa were now driving at a
leisurely speed through thinly populated bush country. There were not many other vehicles on the road.
The sun was climbing higher in the eastern sky.

Waichari noticed a bright blue car had appeared
on the rear view mirror. It was moving faster than
they were. The car held no more than casual interest
to him, and he divided his attention between the
road and Wekesa.

'Do you think Chepkube will always be a centre
for *magendo*?'

Closer and closer came the car behind.

'I doubt it. The coffee boom and the disorder in
Uganda cannot last forever. The patience of both the
Uganda and Kenya governments is bound to run
out, then Chepkube will turn back into an ordinary
trading centre, though I don't suppose this genera-
tion will forget it.'

The blue car was trying to overtake them.
Waichari noticed there were two Arabs in it and he
moved to one side to give them more room to pass by.

But they seemed to be in no hurry to overtake.

'I wish these fellows would make up their minds whether they want to overtake us or not,' Waichari complained, irritated by the other car, which was now driving abreast of them. He could see its occupants clearly now. One was quite old and the driver was young. They were looking at the two friends, and there was something menacing about them.

Menacing! The idea struck Waichari and Wekesa at the same time, but it was too late. Their alarm turned to terror as the older Arab – who was closer on the passenger seat – produced a grenade from his pocket and pulled the pin from it with his teeth. Waichari gave a cry of dismay. There was no time to think, let alone to take evasive action. Waichari's animal instinct of survival took over and he swerved the steering-wheel sharply towards the other car, just as the attacker raised the grenade and aimed.

The two cars collided with a deep, crushing noise, stunning their passengers. The Arabs' car was butted right off the road, and in the process Waichari lost control of his damaged car and it went lumbering forward. There was a terrific explosion in the attackers' car and it burst into flames.

Waichari's car came to a jarring halt and he lay still for a while. As consciousness returned, he realised he was lying on the steering wheel, and his forehead, elbow and back were aching. Wekesa was groaning beside him, with a torn cheek.

Waichari opened the door with difficulty and stood swaying on his feet like a drunkard, gaping at the other car as it burned beside the road. The grenade thrower was burning in the car, past help, but the driver had been half thrown out; his legs were still in the car. He appeared to be half conscious, for he was screaming soundlessly.

It appeared to Waichari to be wicked to watch another human being roast alive, no matter what he had done, and he staggered to the car slowly, for his battered limbs would not permit him to move quickly. He held the young man by his shoulders and dragged him clear of the car. Miraculously, his torso had only minor injuries, but his legs had been mutilated by the grenade.

No sooner had Waichari dragged the man away than another violent explosion rocked the burning car. Waichari flung himself on the grass and gaped as the flames of the car became a blaze. His stunned mind somehow managed to reason out that the car had had another grenade in it, and the petrol tank had yet to go up. He was right. There was yet another explosion and a flash of fire, and the blaze became even more fierce. Little was going to remain of the car and the grenade thrower. This was his funeral pyre.

Waichari could not help remembering that this was the way his parents had died, and he shuddered with horror.

Wekesa had staggered out of his car, and like Waichari, he stood watching the blazing car in numbed silence. After a while he came to his senses.

'We've got to get away from here!' he said urgently.

Waichari looked at him and he came to his senses also. 'I knew it!' he said angrily. 'I knew there was a catch behind your offer to help me. You wanted me to be killed with you. Just let me get my hands on you...!'

98

'Believe me, I did not expect this. I can't see why anyone would want to kill us this way. Why not check if that man can talk?'

They went to the young man. He seemed to have great endurance, for he was still half conscious. They made him as comfortable as possible.

'Just listen...,' Waichari told him. 'You tried to kill us, but I saved you. Why did you try to kill us? We have not harmed you.'

'You are... wicked smugglers,' he finally managed to say. 'Major Mulindwa ... and the chief ... want you dead.'

'Which chief?' Waichari asked.

But the young man could say no more; he was unconscious.

'Let's leave him. He'll survive if help gets here soon, but we won't survive if we stay here any longer. Look! There are two vehicles coming over there.'

They rushed to their smashed car, which had to be abandoned, picked up their papers, guns and all pocketable belongings, and hurried into the bush.

'What do you know of Major Mulindwa and the "chief"?' Waichari turned to ask Wekesa.

'I know the major by reputation,' Wekesa replied uneasily. 'A more bloodthirsty vampire would be hard to find.'

'Exactly what have you done to deserve a grenade? Search your conscience and tell me the truth.'

Wekesa searched his mind and voiced what he suspected he had done. His explanation was incredible, but Waichari believed it, and it alarmed him as much as the grenade had done.

'What do you think we should do?' Waichari

asked. He sounded as uneasy as he felt.

'We should do what they least suspect. But for the present we'll look for one of my friends around here to hide us before they start looking for us.'

The two companions continued hurriedly through the bush, planning.


'The blundering, incompetent fools!' Major Mulindwa cursed, pacing about the room in fury.

When an hour had passed without any form of report from the operatives the major had become apprehensive and sent out a signal to all police stations in the area where the contrabandists were supposed to have been cornered. A report had arrived half an hour later, stating that the operatives had both died in a crash with a Kenyan registered Ford Escort KQF 325.

The major had listened in fury and dismay, then he had ordered police stations and border posts to look out for the culprits. They were to be shot on sight.

The phone rang and the major picked it up, trembling for he knew who was at the other end, and what he wanted.

'What is going on, Major?' snapped the chief. 'Why haven't I had a report?'

'I am afraid the operatives failed, sir,' the major said, and proceeded to report what had occurred.

The chief became as furious as the major had been. 'You brainless baboon! Can't you have anything done right? It appears that nothing can be done correctly unless I supervise it myself. I am coming over. In the meantime, have the border sealed and the area combed for the smugglers.'

'I've already sent out the instructions.'

'I'm surprised you can think of anything by yourself,' the chief said coldly, and hung up.


Wekesa and Waichari hid in a village where the former had friends. They dressed their wounds and took lunch there. The peasants were sympathetic to them since they, too, had been the victims of terrorists serving Amin's dictatorial government. Knowing very well they were being hunted, they stayed in the village for several hours, but they had a journey to make and Wekesa persuaded one of his friends, who had an old pick-up, to drive them to Kampala.

The pick-up was loaded with a few bananas, which were to be the pretext for going to Kampala in case they were stopped. The two friends were disguised as peasant farmers. At half past four they got into the pick-up and drove off in a westerly direction, knowing they were being looked for along the border in the east. They used the least used roads, and they did not meet those who were looking for them. When they reached a main road, they passed army vehicles, but none took undue interest in them and they reached Kampala without being challenged. The owner of the pick-up left them on top of one of the hills of the city, refused to wait for them and returned the way he had come. The time was now six thirty and the city lights were being lit.

Wekesa looked at one of some excellent residential houses below them and said, 'His car is not there so he is not in the house. Let us hope we don't have long to wait. Look, there is a guard as I expected. Remember the plan. We move as soon as he appears.'

They looked for a hidden spot, sat down and waited, watching the house.

Two hours later, a gleaming white limousine approached the house. The guard opened the gate and saluted, and the car drove into the garage. An army officer got out of the car and walked to the front door of the house, which a woman opened for him.

'Note the uniform,' Wekesa said grimly. 'It confirms my suspicion beyond reasonable doubt.'

The friends looked at each other, stood up and walked down to the street where the house was. Making sure there were no onlookers nearby, they walked casually along until they came alongside the house.

The guard eyed them suspiciously because of their rough appearance, but he did not know they were a threat until it was too late.

The two friends whipped out pistols and pointed them at the horrified guard.

'Open the gate,' Wekesa snapped, 'or we'll just climb over and walk on your carcass. Don't make a sound.'

The guard turned towards the house, his eyes rolling in fright. Seeing Wekesa raise his gun, he changed his mind about shouting and opened the gate.

Working swiftly, the two friends bound and gagged the man, then walked up to the front door. It was not locked and they twisted the knob and got inside, their guns held forward.

In the spacious sitting room was an elderly, be-spectacled, slightly-built army officer of high rank, who had a glass of Nubian gin in his hand. Serving him was a healthy young woman in one of the long, national dresses called *busuuti*. They both looked up in fright and dismay. The army officer was none other than Mr Sowedi, the pleasant Kampala businessman Waichari and Wekesa had visited a week earlier.

'Who? Why? What?' Sowedi began, then stared in fascinated horror as he recognised the intruders.

'Shut up and put your hands up,' Wekesa snapped, and proceeded to relieve Sowedi of a holstered gun.

Waichari made an inspection of the house, from which he returned covering a frightened male servant with his gun. Working swiftly, he proceeded to bind and gag him and the woman, while Wekesa covered them and kept warning them not to make a sound.

Sowedi had overcome his shock and adopted an air of anger. 'I demand an explanation for this outrage,' he said.

'We have no time to fool about with you, Mr Sowedi, or should we call you Chief?' asked Waichari.

'Chief?' Sowedi became more amazed. 'What are you talking...?'

'I warned you, we have no time, Mr Chief of Operations. We know everything, so you can put off your act. We want our colleague and fellow country-man, Mr Njogu, dead or alive. If he is restored to us alive and well, then we have no quarrel with you. But if he is dead, we are going to execute you.'

'You must be mad!' Sowedi began. 'I told you

Njogu was in Rwanda. He arrived in the morning but you failed to come and meet him as I instructed you. Right now his convoy is on its...'

Before he could continue, Waichari slapped him, breaking his glasses and sending him cowering against the wall. Half blinded by the blow and lack of glasses, Sowedi studied Waichari's blurred face with its lean, hard features and narrowed eyes, with hate and fear. Waichari grabbed Sowedi's jacket and jerked him upright.

'You can't bluff us again, mister.' Waichari's low voice was hard and cold. 'We want Njogu, dead or alive, for he is not going to be one of those who disappear mysteriously under your bloody regime.'

'I tell you I don't know what you...'

'Some people never learn,' Waichari interrupted, shaking his head. 'Perhaps you should refresh his mind, Wekesa. Tell him all that we know he has done, and what made us suspect him.'

'My suspicions began when I didn't hear from Njogu for two weeks,' Wekesa began. 'He normally keeps in contact with me. I phoned your depot twice, Sowedi, but each time your secretary brushed me off with vague explanations. I became uneasy and decided to come personally. That was when I met Waichari here. He looked like the sort of man I needed in my mission. I made inquiries about him, and they confirmed my opinion.'

'I can also be nasty,' Waichari added, piercing the dizzy Sowedi with narrowed eyes, 'but I am giving you a chance to give us information voluntarily.'

Waichari put the guns in a corner. Only one pistol remained in Wekesa's hand, and even this he was ordered not to point at Sowedi. Waichari went on to order them in a quiet voice to sit down.

'How can we relax our vigilance over this snake?' Wekesa protested.

'I said I am giving him a chance,' Waichari explained. 'Now that we are comfortably seated, we can proceed with our discussion.'

Wekesa and Sowedi stared at Waichari as if he was insane, then Wekesa continued, 'My unease was increased when we were tailed by two men on our way here. They had also watched my movements at the Nairobi flat. I could think of no explanation, but since I was uneasy, I came here last week with Waichari, and you put us at ease. Goodness knows under what threats you made Njogu sign that note which enabled you to convince us to wait for a week. You told us to return today, thinking that we would be killed on the way. You were clever enough to make sure that Njogu's convoy was seen on the way to Rwanda, in case anyone inquired, which I did at a petrol station.'

'You are mad,' Sowedi said. He had grown calm. Now and then he glanced at the guns in the corner longingly.

'It was the grenade which made everything clear,' Wekesa continued, 'and everything pointed to you, Sowedi. We were attacked while coming to see you. It looked as if you didn't want us to come and ask you more questions about Njogu.'

'Surely that is not sufficient proof of my guilt?' Sowedi asked.

'There is more,' Wekesa replied. 'It was only you who could have known I was dangerous to anyone who tried to get rid of Njogu secretly. I also wondered at your influence over the armed forces when you were only a businessman. Njogu always brought you goods with perfect immunity, even when this country was most chaotic. You had to be something else, so when the Arab talked of a 'Chief', I suspected it to be you. That suspicion became a certainty when Waichari and I saw you in army uniform. It can only have been you who sent spies to observe us and then to eliminate us.'

'Why should I have sent them to do that ?' Sowedi sneered, though he was listening keenly.

'Though most of the top brains of Uganda have been eliminated, you are one of the few left, though you are twisted. People like Major Mulindwa would have just gunned Njogu down and forgotton it, but you pause to think of the repercussions. Njogu has the influence of powerful people who would cause an uproar in the Kenyan Parliament and the press, not to mention the other big shots who still supply goods to Uganda, who would become afraid and stop bringing goods as others did. You would have to close your great business.'

'Why should I harm Njogu?' Sowedi asked. 'He is my friend.'

'Your greed overcame your friendship,' Wekesa explained. 'I know that you owe Njogu half a million shillings, but instead of repaying it, you preferred to make yourself a millionaire by seizing his vehicles as well as the stock of nearly a million shillings he brought on the last trip. You must have explained to your government that you were eliminating him for "economic crimes", but we know it was for personal gain.'

'Such are the grounds for our suspicions,' Waichari concluded for Wekesa. 'The only question that remains is, what did you do with Njogu?'

'These are wild accusations,' Sowedi, replied. 'I deny them.'

'You can keep Njogu's property,' Waichari went on, 'but if there's a spark of humanity left in you, give him, as well as his crew to us. His wife and children are crying for him. I have kept our guns aside so that you may give us this information voluntarily.'

Sowedi stirred in his seat uncomfortably, but said nothing.

'It is as we feared,' Waichari told Wekesa. 'The vampire killed Njogu. Shoot him and let us be gone.'

As Wekesa hesitated, Waichari said he would do the shooting, and grabbed the gun. There was a brief struggle, and the gun fell on the table. Swiftly, Sowedi grabbed the gun and smiled.

'Hands up and keep still, gentlemen,' he said. His usually pleasant voice was chilling.

Waichari and Wekesa obeyed in dismay. 'You have given him the upper hand, Waichari,' Wekesa complained bitterly. 'Now we can expect no mercy.'

'You're right, you can expect no mercy,' Sowedi agreed, still smiling. It was a smile that did not reach his eyes. Last time Waichari had thought Sowedi was a pleasant-looking man, but now that Sowedi had lost his glasses, he could see that his eyes were as fascinating and cold as those of a snake.

'I'll hand you over to the Butcher, and spend a pleasant evening watching him make you scream.'

Sowedi rose to his feet and walked round to where the two friends were seated and gave Waichari a vicious kick in the leg. Waichari winced and gave a suppressed groan.

'That ought to teach you to hit men older than yourself,' Sowedi explained. 'Now to phone Major Mulindwa...'

'Wait,' Wekesa pleaded. 'At least you should tell us about your plan, and what you did with Njogu. You owe us that much.'

'Gladly. You were right. I had Njogu arrested and thrown into the State Research Bureau Head-quarters. But as you put it, he is no simple man. I had to wait and see the reaction from Kenya. At first I thought I could get away with the story that he had gone to Rwanda, but then you started your inquiry by telephone. I sent the Nubians to see how much you suspected, but they bungled, and the major eliminated them. After I had stalled you, my plan to get rid of the big shot with his crew was this: Njogu and his men were to be stabbed, put in some of their vehicles, crashed with a petrol trailer and set aflame, near the Rwanda-Ugandan border. After the holocaust no one could have proved that it was an arranged accident. The newspapers would just call it "the worst motor accident ever". It would have taken place tonight, but I had to stop it when the Arabs failed to eliminate you. But now you have been kind enough to bring yourselves. Fortune has indeed smiled upon me, for now you will be eliminated once and for all, and the operation will go ahead as planned. Ha, ha, ha!' Sowedi laughed heartily.

'Then I take it Njogu is still alive?' Wekesa asked eagerly when the laughter had subsided.

'Yes, though he is not much to look at,' Sowedi replied. 'The major has been amusing himself with him. Now let me call the major to amuse himself with you also.'

'No, you won't,' Waichari said coldly, rising to his feet.

'Sit down, or I shoot!' Sowedi snapped, aiming at Waichari's heart.

As Waichari still came on, Sowedi squeezed the trigger. There was a clicking sound but no explosion. Sowedi tried again and gazed at the gun in dismay.

'You have been tricked, my friend,' Waichari's lazy voice explained. 'The gun is empty. We deliberately let you have it to make you brag and give us the information we wanted, and it worked. It was tidier than torture, don't you think?'

Sowedi was nearly mad with terror and rage. Waichari and Wekesa picked up the guns from against the wall and Wekesa rammed the muzzle of his into Sowedi's back. Sowedi could not believe this was happening to him.

'Mr Sowedi,' Wekesa said grimly, 'we came here to get either Njogu or your life, and we're not leaving without taking one or the other. You're going to have him and his crew released, or we're going to shoot you. We'll leave you dead, return to our country and make the kind of noise you feared and use every kind of pressure possible to have him released. Come on, choose, are you going to release him or are you going to die?'

'How do you expect me to release him? I'd have to go to the Bureau.'

'You can use the telephone. All you need is a plausible story. Say that Waichari and I made it back to Kenya and reported to Njogu's friends in the government. Say the government of Kenya has appealed to the Big Man, and the Big Man himself has ordered his release. I am sure that none would question an order from the Big Man.'

'I can't do that!' Sowedi said in fear. 'If the Big Man finds out I gave such an order pretending it came from him, I'd face the firing squad.'

'Maybe. All that I'm certain about is that I'll blow your brains out if you don't pick up that telephone and start talking, without trying any tricks. The prisoners are to be escorted to the border and set free.'

Sowedi was reluctant to obey, but he could see Wekesa meant what he said and his instinct of survival forced him to pick up the phone and ring the major.

'Major? Chief here. Bad news. Those meddlesome contrabandists have gone back to Kenya and raised hell. The Minister of Foreign Affairs has contacted the Big Man himself, and he has ordered the immediate release of the prisoners. So I am afraid the operation is at an end. I want you to carry all the prisoners to the border in a lorry and set them free immediately.'

The major was outraged. 'But, sir, how can we release them after all the trouble we've undergone? What happens when the big shot starts yelling for his property?'

'We'll deny all knowledge of the property, Major. Anyhow, who are you to question an order from the Big Man?'

'Okay, sir, if you'll just come over and sign their release.'

'You may sign on my behalf for I'll be busy elsewhere until morning. In the meantime, the prisoners must be across the border by midnight, understand?'

After a pause the major said reluctantly, 'Yes, sir.' He started to add something, changed his mind and hung up.

Sowedi turned to Wekesa. 'I've done all I could. Pray that the major isn't smart enough to call the Big Man for confirmation, or to come here to check if everything is all right.'

The two friends held a brief consultation, then they locked up the guard, the woman and the servant in one of the bedrooms, and forced Sowedi into his limousine.

'You intend to murder me after all!' he complained bitterly.

'You are our ticket out of Kampala,' Wekesa replied. 'We're getting away in your car. You're driving, for no one would stop an army colonel. But if there is trouble, you'll bluff our way through, for there will be a gun in your ribs all the time. Give us away or make the slightest mistake and you'll be beef before you realise it.'

Sowedi glared at them with hatred, but he did as he was told. Wekesa was right. No one stopped the army officer and they made it to the forest area near the border, where they hid the car in the bush and crossed the border on foot, using one of the bush tracks used by smugglers and cattle raiders. Once across, they sat down to wait for daylight, for Sowedi was not going to be released until the major had been given enough time to release the prisoners.

As the sat in the bush, Waichari was filled with gloom. The day's adventures made it impossible for him to return to Uganda on another smuggling trip. He had known all the time that his luck had been too good to last. He still had a considerable sum to raise, and there were only two days to go to the auction.

# Chapter 10

At dawn Waichari and Wekesa released their prisoner and walked to the border post. There they met a customs official and two policemen who informed them that Njogu and his crew had been released an hour earlier. They had been brought to the border in a tipper.

'They were in a pitiful shape. They seemed to have been subjected to constant starvation and torture. They were the remains of the men they had once been,' he told them.

Wekesa looked uneasily at Waichari and asked the official, 'Did you see their boss?'

The officer nodded. 'I am afraid he was in the worst shape. He was unconscious and had to be carried on a stretcher.'

'Where are they?'

'In Bungoma District Hospital. When I saw the condition in which they were, I instructed the driver of my Land-Rover to rush them to the hospital without more ado.'

Wekesa turned to Waichari and said, 'Come on, man, there is no time to be lost.'

After thanking the official, the two friends walked to their lodging in Chepkube, where Mutua and the boys were waiting anxiously for them with the lorry load of foodstuff. After all the couple had done in

Uganda, they would be completely mad to return there. How were they going to dispose of the food-stuff? How was Waichari going to raise the remaining capital for the loan? Time was running out! But even with these pressing problems, the sick man came first.

The friends took hasty showers, changed their clothes and ate breakfast. Then they hired a car and made for the hospital, which lay about ninety kilometres north-east of Chepkube.

At the outpatients' department of the hospital they met Njogu's crew. They were in a pitiful condition, as the customs official had said. They were feeble and their battered bodies were wasted, giving one the impression of scarecrows or walking skeletons. But they managed weak smiles when they saw Wekesa, and shook hands with him and his companion.

'How did you know we were here?' the foreman asked.

'I learned at the border post.'

'Did you know that we were imprisoned in the dreaded State Research Bureau all the time?'

'I suspected it, but I didn't know for certain until yesterday.'

'We couldn't believe it was happening to us. A jeep-load of soldiers stopped our convoy outside Kampala. This was normal, but they claimed the papers the boss showed them were not in order. He tried to reason with them, but it was all in vain, for they were determined to arrest us. We were ordered at gunpoint to get into another jeep they had with them, and presently we were inside the building in Nakasero. There they started tormenting us with senseless interrogations. They mutilated us with knives, smashed our toes with hammers and...' He broke down with emotion.

'We thought we were doomed,' the foreman went on.

'We thought we were going to be murdered last night, and we were sure of it when we were loaded into a blood-spattered tipper. It is impossible to be more terrified than we were. It came to us as a shock when we were dumped at the border and told to go home. We couldn't believe we were free.'

'Even now we are still puzzled,' another driver put in. 'The Butcher had been awaiting our execution with anticipation. What made him suddenly change his mind and release us? Mr Wekesa, you claim you knew of our predicament yesterday. Were you in any way instrumental in our release?'

'Perhaps, but I wouldn't have managed it without the assistance of my friend here. He is Mr Waichari Mathu.'

Waichari was uncomfortable at the sheer gratitude the men poured on him and Wekesa, but he thought it was worth the risk they had taken in going to rescue them.

'How did you manage it?' the foreman asked.

'Never mind that now. It is not of much importance. I might tell you some other time. Right now we want to see Mr Njogu. Where is he?'

The foreman's face clouded with worry. 'He was taken to that ward over there. It is no use seeing him now. He has been unconscious for the last four days.'

Wekesa looked at Waichari's grim face, then at the foreman. 'We'll inquire all the same. I'll see you after you're treated and give you money for food and for your transport home as soon as possible.'

Unhappily, the two friends walked over to the ward the foreman had indicated to them. The doctor was standing in the doorway, looking tired and unhappy. The friends had a feeling there was bad news in store for them, and it was Waichari who had the courage to ask the question they dreaded most.

'How is he, doctor?'

The doctor shook his head. 'We've done all we could for him,' he said, avoiding looking directly into their eyes, 'but I am afraid he has lost too much blood and suffered too much pain. This has weakened him greatly, and the unhygenic conditions under which his numerous wounds have been kept have reduced his resistance to pneumonia which...' He shook his head again. 'But even now we've revived him sufficiently for him to talk. You may talk to him for three minutes, but no more. Don't excite him in any way.'

The two looked at each other with hope, but that hope was to be shattered when they walked into the ward and the nurse drew the curtains surrounding Njogu's bed. They looked down at the dark, mutilated face. It looked lifeless, but the chest was rising and falling faintly. It was the same man whose tissue the Butcher had cut.

Wekesa almost wept in his distress. 'Njogu,' he called softly.

As if by a miracle, Njogu's eyes opened slightly. They looked blank. Wekesa called him again and slowly the sick man recognised the hazy faces looking anxiously down at him.

'Wekesa... Waichari... ' he whispered. 'How...? Where...?'

116

'You're in hospital in Western Kenya, Mr Njogu,' said Wekesa. 'Waichari and I had you released from Uganda. Never mind how.'

The sick man tried to smile and only succeeded with a grim face. 'I knew... you would... come. Thank you... even if... it is... too late.'

Waichari felt they were running out of time already, and what had to be said had to be said fast. 'Your wife and your sons sent me to find you, Njogu, to inform you that they miss you. Maina says he can recite the alphabet.'

Sorrow clouded Njogu's face. 'Tell them... I miss them too... when it is... too late. Hope to meet them... in a better world. I go to my grave... repentant.'

Njogu's eyes closed, but they opened again after a while. 'Waichari, old pal... don't do *magendo*. Stay poor, but alive. I made a fortune... but now I am... dying.'

'Please don't talk of death. You'll make it,' Wekesa pleaded.

After another pause, Njogu continued, 'I am going... you know it. I had foreseen... something like this might happen. See my lawyer. Everything goes... to my wife... in trust for my sons. You Wekesa... will be my business trustee. Let my sons... grow up to meet... their heritage intact.'

Njogu had spoken with great effort, and having said these words he closed his eyes and became unconscious. He did not recover consciousness again and he passed away peacefully two hours later.

That night the two friends tried to drown their sorrow in drink. But there was no escape from their

117

grief. They kept talking about the virtues of the dead man between intervals of silence.

'I don't want the death to be announced for the time being,' Wekesa said. 'I want the news to be broken to Mrs Njogu first. Also we've got the other urgent matter of saving your property, or have you forgotten?'

'How can I forget?' Waichari complained bitterly. 'It is only one day to go to the auction bell. This affair has shattered any hope I had of raising the remaining sum.'

'How much is it?'

'I have eighty thousand in cash and a hundred thousand in stock, so I am thirty thousand short – forty thousand to be more realistic, because of the costs. It is still too much money to be raised in one day. I don't see any way, short of selling the lorry, painful as it would be, for I have given up *magendo* for good.'

Waichari rose to his feet with his glass and stood looking into the night without really seeing anything. 'I thought I'd rather die than face bankruptcy,' he murmured, 'but now that I've seen the mischance of those who practise *magendo*, I have decided that there are worse things than poverty. In Chepkube I have seen human greed at its worst.' Waichari's mind flashed back to the time he had seen a carpenter lift his hammer to crush a man's skull. 'These people are prepared to leave their jobs and their families and to kill because of money. I shan't be one of them any longer. I thought I came here to save my honour, but surely there can be no worse degradation than to sacrifice my soul on this nasty altar of greed. From now onwards I'll solve my problems by more regular methods, even if I lose property and friends in the process.'

'I understand,' was all Wekesa commented.

Waichari emptied his glass and paced about the room, hard in thought. Then he turned to his companion.

'I can think of no way of raising the cash I need, but at least we can turn that foodstuff we bought in Kitale into cash. Let us go and look for Ayub.'

They did find the Ugandan contrabandist, just as he was leaving the back room of the bar where they normally negotiated. The man did not welcome them as warmly as he usually did, for he was vexed.

'It's about time you fellows turned up,' he said. 'Are you aware that I wasted the whole of last night waiting for you? Do you think you are the only customers for my goods? If you think I've got nothing better to do than await your pleasure, then you have another thought coming.'

'Calm down, Ayub,' Wekesa said in a coaxing manner, and went on to explain the circumstances which had kept them in Uganda throughout the night before. As Ayub listened, it was obvious that he did not trust them, and it took him some moments to believe that they were talking the truth. He studied the two men for while. 'So Mr Njogu is dead?' He shook his head sympathetically, then asked, 'What are you going to do now?'

'There is little we can do,' Waichari told him. 'We dare not cross the border again to get your coffee, or we'd lose our lives and the lorry. I wish to request you to buy the foodstuff I have amassed, even if I can't buy your coffee in return.'

'How do you expect me to transport the stuff if I

119

don't use your lorry?' He sounded aggrieved.

Waichari turned to Wekesa. 'Surely you can find him a vehicle?'

Wekesa thought for a moment. 'Perhaps. The trouble is that none is available right now. You must have noticed that, in Chepuke, all lorries and pick-ups are absent on business during the night. We can only wait for daylight when they return.'

'I can't afford to wait for tomorrow,' Waichari said uneasily. 'By then it will be too late. Can't Ayub find somewhere to store the stuff until he finds a lorry?'

'A store for so much foodstuff at a moment's notice?' Ayub inquired, shaking his head. 'I am afraid you'll have to do as Wekesa suggests and wait for tomorrow.'

Since Waichari had no choice but to wait for daylight, he wondered how on earth he was going to unload the foodstuff and make it back home in time to pay the loan. He also wondered how he was going to raise the remaining money.

These questions and others kept preying on his mind and made him unable to sleep when they went back to their room. He could do nothing but lie awake thinking and studying the ceiling, hoping the new day would bring better counsel.


When daylight came, Wekesa found a lorry as big as Waichari's. The vehicles were parked back to back and the long, tedious task of stock-taking and unloading began. It was not over until lunch time, and by then Waichari had not yet thought of a way to raise the two thousand pounds he still required. Wekesa had no idea either. Time had run out anyhow. It was too late to drive back home and pay the loan, even if he managed to raise the money. While Wekesa and the crew sat down to lunch, Waichari sat staring at a wall vacantly, feeling sick. Already he could see the autioneer saying, 'Going, going, gone! To Mr Kanyi,' and the oval face of a young girl with feeling eyes. He could also see his sister, her thin face filled with hate. She would never forgive him for as long as she lived. And all for two thousand pounds! No, it was not even to be contemplated. He was going to fight on to the last moment.

In his desperation, Waichari thought the best thing to do was to talk to the bank manager and plead with him to give him time to raise the remaining sum. The trouble was that Waichari knew very well that the man was encouraging Kanyi to buy the property.

'It's certainly worth a try,' Wekesa encouraged him when he heard of Waichari's idea.

They hurried to Kanji Shah's store, where they put a call through to the bank. When it was through, Waichari asked for the manager.

'Hello, what can I do for you?' the manager asked.

'Hello. This is Waichari Mathu speaking. I am calling you to inform you I am now in a position to clear eighty per cent of my debt, plus costs.'

'You are?' the manager asked, with some surprise.

'Yes. I request you to ask your lawyer to stop the auction until I see him in the morning.'

There was a pause, then the manager said, 'I am afraid it is impossible to stop the proceedings. Not unless you settle accounts with our lawyers today and in full, for the auctioneer will have had his instructions for tomorrow. Anyhow, I am not supposed to be discussing this with you. Consult the lawyer.'

Waichari did not like the sound of that, and he said pleadingly, 'I can't make it today, but I promise to be there first thing in the morning. I believe you are the only one who can help me. Once you told me it is your duty to guard public money. I feel you would not be failing in it if you granted me a little time in the morning, and accepted what I have. If I have raised so much, surely I have proved I can raise the remaining amount? You will not be failing the public if you grant me this request, and I shall be eternally grateful.'

'For the last time, Mr Mathu, I advise you to consult our lawyer.'

Waichari was getting irritated by these words, but he didn't let it affect his voice as he went on pleading with the man. Handling people with care saves a lot of trouble, except, of course, when one is reasoning with those who are like oxes or bricks.

'You know the circumstances under which I got saddled with this debt. I didn't expect it, and I want to clear it above everything else. I am also responsible for two students. It is now just a year since we lost our parents. It would be disastrous for us to lose our home now. Since you won't be failing the public by granting my request, sir, I beg you to do so on humanitarian grounds.'

There was a long pause, then the manager said, 'I'll consult our lawyer. See him in the morning.'

Waichari sighed with relief. The man was human after all and, though he was a friend of Kanyi, it seemed he had nothing personal against Waichari.

'Thank you very much, sir. I won't fail you.'

Waichari put the receiver down, his face looking less worried than it had been all morning.

# Chapter 11

At nine-thirty on the morning of the day of the auction, a crowd was gathered at the car park of Waichari's farm. There were a few vehicles belonging to prospective buyers, and one of them was Kanyi's station wagon. From the parking place, there was a perfect view of the productive farm down to the valley below. The enormous Kanyi was in a jovial mood, and he discussed politics and joked with the other prospective buyers.

The sun was climbing the eastern sky, and people were looking forward to the arrival of the auctioneers. The auction was to take place at ten. Some of the people were discussing the value of the farm, with its coffee, paddocks and half-built house. Few were sympathetic, for people tend to take other people's problems lightly.

The few who were genuinely sympathetic were in the sitting-room of the house below the parking place, comforting Waitherero and Muna. Waitherero was beyond help though, and she sat with her head bent, unmoved by whatever the comforters were saying.

'If the worst comes to worst, Muna,' said a young man, 'you can stay in my place. Your schooling must not be disrupted.'

'Waitherero can stay at mine,' said a quiet voice at

the doorway. Waitherero looked up in surprise. It was her friend Janet who had spoken, she whom she had thought was far away in another district. She was simply attired but looked beautiful, though her oval face was sad.

'Janet,' said Waitherero gratefully. If there was anyone she needed most at this moment, it was her friend. 'You've come at last. Where have you been all this time? Come into my room and tell me all your news.'

The two friends went into Waitherero's room and sat on the bed. Through the window one could see the proceedings outside the house. Another car was arriving. It was probably that of the auctioneers. The crowd was growing larger and noisier. Mr Kanyi was getting impatient for the auction to begin, and he kept glancing at his watch. The time was ten minutes to ten, and still the auctioneers had not arrived.

'So your brother has not yet returned?'

'No.'

'Have you any idea where he is?'

'I haven't.' Waitherero started sniffing. Janet turned to her, and Waitherero was surprised to fin i that her friend's eyes were moist as if she, too, was on the verge of tears. They held one another and fell silent, seeming to derive comfort from each other's contact. There was no need for words.

Ten o'clock came and still the auctioneers had not arrived. People started complaining aloud. Kanyi's high-pitched voice was more furious than the rest.

The sound of an approaching heavy vehicle came to them and Waitherero listened keenly. Her face brightened. 'That is our lorry. Waichari is here!'

Sure enough, the sound came closer and closer. Then Waichari's big lorry appeared and steered into the farm. People made way for it and told one another who it was. Then they fell silent as it stopped. Three ragged men appeared from the cab while the two turn-boys jumped from the rear. All eyes were on the tall, slim one, who wore a hat and carried a suitcase.

'You're right!' Janet gasped. 'It is your brother.'

For a while, Waichari stood studying the crowd grimly and silently. A few greeted him, and he acknowledged the greetings with a nod. Then he led his companions to the house in his unhurried manner.

'He is here, but can he rescue us?' Waitherero wondered, and led her friend back into the dining-room. Presently Waichari and his companions came in and shook hands with those in the room. He smiled sadly as he shook hands with Waitherero.

'Good morning, little sister. Can you prepare something for my companions? This one is Wekesa, a very good friend.'

Waitherero shook hands with Wekesa and welcomed him, but her attention was on Waichari. 'Where have you been?' she asked him. 'Are you aware how anxious we've been? Did you succeed?'

Waichari held up his hand. 'Peace, sister. First I want some water to wash my face, and refreshments for my men, then perhaps I can get around to answering...'

Waichari stopped. His heart missed a beat and he felt a tremor inside his body. He had noticed Janet. He had expected her to be gone. It was a relief to see her and to know she had not forsaken them after all, during their darkest hour. But his relief was short-lived.

'How are you, Waruguru?'

'I am very well, thank you,' she replied politely.

'I am pleased to see you are still around. How is everyone at home?'

'They are all right.'

Once again, Waichari was hurt by her coldness. What was it that Waitherero had told him over the phone about her? It was something to do with his having wronged her in a way for which she could not forgive him. What had he done? He would get her to tell him at the earliest possible moment. Waichari did not show his feelings as he regarded her, but talked with a politeness that matched her own. 'Greet them for me when you get back.' Then he turned to Wekesa.

'Take a seat, man, I won't be long.'

'So this is your place,' Wekesa said. 'It really is worthwhile. Now I understand your determination to fight for it.'

Waitherero called Janet and they both disappeared into the kitchen while Waichari went to the bathroom, seemingly indifferent to the crowd near the house. By the time he had changed his clothing, the girls were serving milk and peas with potatoes. Waichari took the food and washed it down with a mug of the milk.

Someone cleared his throat and said, 'You haven't yet told us where you've been all this time, Waichari, and what is going to happen now.' The man gestured in the direction of the crowd.

Waichari held up his hand. 'Peace. I will explain later,' he said, rising in his slow motion manner.

'Right now, Wekesa and I have another matter to attend to.'

He turned to Mutua and the turn-boys. 'I wish to congratulate you for your hard work and cooperation. Take a rest and report on Monday. There is much we must do.' He gazed at Janet as if appealing for her to wait, but there was no response. He shrugged his shoulders and nodded to Wekesa and they both walked out.

The crowd in the parking place fell silent as Waichari approached. He stopped before them. 'I hate to disappoint you, but the kind of party you were expecting has been postponed indefinitely. The organisers send their regrets.'

People looked at each other, then voiced their disappointment and disbelief. 'It is a trick!' Kanyi's girlish voice said above the rest.

'Don't take my word for it, then,' said Waichari. 'You can all wait and bask in the sun for as long as you like.' Waichari's eyes narrowed as they turned to Kanyi. 'All except you, Mr Kanyi. I thought I made it quite clear this place is out of bounds for you.'

'How dare you talk to me like that?'

'Because you're trespassing again.'

As Waichari walked to his pick-up, Kanyi realised, much as he feared to admit it, that there really was to be no auction! But it was not possible! Kanyi said to himself. He had spent too much time planning to get the farm. Missing it now was a frustration not to be contemplated. 'He can't have paid!' Kanyi moaned aloud. 'He must have stolen the money!'

Waichari heard him and moved away from the

pick-up towards the big man menacingly.

'You'll apologise, mister,' Waichari hissed through clenched teeth. 'Or you'll find yourself in the intensive care unit of the nearest hospital.'

'My tongue slipped,' Kanyi said.

Waichari grabbed Kanyi by the coat, but then thought better of it and roughly shook him free, saying, 'Pah, you're not even worth wasting time on.'

Waichari shoved the man away with such force that Kanyi went staggering backwards and sat in the dust. The indignity of it made people giggle and Kanyi more furious. Waichari turned away from him and went to his pick-up where he joined Wekesa. Waichari turned the ignition key, raced the engine a few times, then they were off towards the west, leaving Kanyi cursing in his humiliation.

They had left Chepkube during the evening and travelled all night with a few stops. When the bank's attorney had opened his office in the morning, he had found them waiting. Waichari had paid all but a thousand shillings of the money he had, and he had been very happy and grateful when the attorney had phoned the auctioneers and cancelled the auction. In his relief Waichari had taken his companions to a snack bar in the district headquarters, where they had taken drinks in celebration.

'That's one unpleasant task taken care of,' said Waichari as the pick-up sped them up into the hilly bush country. 'Now for the next.'


Half an hour later they drove up to Njogu's home. The housemaid and two little boys came to meet them. They smiled their welcomes.

'It is the uncle who was here,' the elder of the children said.

'Yes, it is Maina,' said Waichari as he shook hands with them. 'I am glad you still remember me.'

'Did you find Daddy? Did you tell him I can count and recite the alphabet?' Waichari nodded. 'Was he pleased? When is he coming to listen to me and to reward me?'

Waichari and Wekesa exchanged disturbed glances.

'Er... your father has gone on a journey, Maina.' Waichari turned to the maid. 'Where is their mother?'

'She is teaching, but she will be in for lunch presently. Do come in and sit down.'

As the friends entered the house, the small boy kept making them uncomfortable with questions.

'Where did he go? When will he be back?'

They were saved from answering by the sounds of an approaching car. 'It's Mummy!' the children cried, hurrying from the house, forgetting their father for the moment.

Mrs Njogu was happy to see her visitors, and she shook their hands warmly. 'Waichari! Wekesa! So you two did meet. I wasn't expecting to see you so soon, but I am very glad.'

'We are also glad to see you and the children again,' Waichari said politely.

It was not long before she surmised from their manner that something was wrong. She asked what was the matter. The two men hesitated then, as gently as he could, Waichari told her.

'Whaat?' she exclaimed in disbelief. When she

realised they were serious, her face contorted with dismay, then became stricken with shock. She sank into a chair and lowered her face into her hands, and stayed that way for a long time.

After some time Waichari told her of the circumstances which had led her husband to his death. She listened in silence, still looking numb.

'I also feared something like this would happen,' she said, 'but I find it hard to believe now that it has happened. I have always begged him to stop going to Uganda until there was peace there, but he was always after making more and more wealth. I wish he had remained a bank manager. I wished him to be more homely than rich. That is why I sent you to him, Waichari. It seems you arrived too late.'

'He was sincerely sorry,' Waichari told her. 'At the last moment he said he missed you three, and would go to his grave repentant. He said he hoped to meet you in a better world. His last words were for the well-being of his sons, so please don't think he was indifferent to them.'

'Thank goodness for that.'

'We share your sorrow with you,' Wekesa told her, 'and you can rely on us during this dark hour. First we have to think of the funeral. As for his business affairs, I think we should discuss them after we have laid him to rest. Do you agree, Mama?'

'He always trusted you with his affairs, Wekesa,' said Jane Njogu, 'and I think I'll rely on you to make the best arrangements. I can't think for myself at the moment.'

They discussed the funeral arrangements, though Jane still could not believe they were for her husband. Then, after comforting her and promising to see her on Monday, they left her to get used to the idea that she was a widow.

As the two friends sped away, Wekesa said, 'I am glad that that has been taken care of. I am afraid I can't stop at your place. I've got some urgent business in town.'

'I'll take you there, but I won't stop, for I've also got an urgent matter to take care of,' Waichari replied, thinking of Janet.

After he had taken Wekesa to town and returned home later on in the evening, he found the girl had gone. His only consolation was to see that his sister looked happy for once, and treated him with respect.

As she served him a drink she said, 'You haven't confirmed whether the ordeal is over. I cannot believe it is.'

'If you mean the loan problem, a little of it is still there, but with hard work and good luck, we shall overcome it. You still don't have confidence in me?'

'I have... a little.' She lowered her face. 'Perhaps I have been too harsh on you.'

'Some day, little sister, perhaps you'll learn not to condemn people too hastily and vehemently, but to try and be more understanding. Sometimes people get into misfortunes in circumstances beyond their control.'

'Still, I find it hard to understand how you got into such a big debt.'

Muna, who was leaning against the front door, said, 'Unlike you and Janet, I trust Waichari.' Muna came from the doorway and into the room. He looked hard at Waichari. 'I don't see how he could have made such a blunder. He hasn't been wasting much money. I have been thinking, and the only way we could have got into such a debt was...'

'Ssh! Keep your thoughts to yourself,' Waichari told him. The boy, being intelligent, had guessed the truth about their father, but Waichari had long decided to shoulder the blame, no matter how unpleasant it was. 'I know what you're thinking, Muna, and you're wrong. Don't let me ever hear you mention it.'

Muna stared at him doubtfully, then shrugged his shoulders. 'All right, I won't mention it, though I don't see how else we got into the mess.' He was touched by Waichari's nobility.

'What are you two talking about?' Waitherero asked, looking from one to the other.

'Forget it,' Waichari told her. 'Tell me when your friend left.'

'She left after everyone else, at two in the afternoon. She told me to tell you she is very glad you've saved our home, and to say goodbye. She is leaving to start her secretarial course first thing in the morning.'

Waichari felt gloomy and disappointed. There had been a faint ray of hope when he had seen her that morning: now it was gone.

Before he let her go, however, there was a little matter he wanted to clear up with her. Something he couldn't understand about her. 'Waitherero, would you please go to her place and persuade her to drop in here before she goes away? Tell her I want to escort her to the bus stop, even if I know I've annoyed her.'

'Right.' Waitherero was distressed by Waichari's tone. She had never known him to sound pleading. She set off for Janet's place immediately.

Finishing his drink, Waichari went to his room to lie down and think of what he would tell Janet, if she did come in the morning.

Waichari awoke at sunrise next morning. He washed, shaved and dressed carefully for once while Muna washed the pick-up and Waitherero prepared breakfast. After some persuasion, Janet had told Waitherero she might drop in at six thirty am. But by seven, when they were taking breakfast, she had not come.

'If she doesn't come,' Waichari thought, 'I won't pursue her.'

Janet did come presently, but she seemed to be in a hurry. She knocked on the door and stood at the doorway.

'Good morning, everyone,' she said in her quiet way. 'I am going now for I've got some shopping to do in the town before I go to the college, and the Principal is expecting me at ten.'

Pretending to gaze at her as casually as she was studying him, Waichari devoured her with his eyes. She was looking smarter and lovelier than usual. Once again, Waichari felt a tremor inside him. It really was a pity she was walking out of his life.

'There is no need for you to worry about time,' he told her. 'I've decided to drive you there myself.'

She regarded him not gratefully but gravely. 'Thank you. But you really must not put yourself to so much trouble on my account.'

'For goodness sake, Waruguru, why are you treating him like a stranger?' Waitherero exclaimed impatiently. 'Of course you'll be more comfortable in the pick-up than in an overloaded *matatu*. If you won't take coffee, then let's see you off.'

'Excellent idea,' Waichari said, taking Janet's suitcase.

Janet looked at him unkindly but she did not protest. She followed the family to the pick-up. Waichari secured her suitcase at the back and stood holding the passenger door open for her. The girls embraced. They were genuinely sorry to part.

After saying goodbye to Muna, Janet got into the pick-up and Waichari slammed the door shut. Then he went round to the driver's door. He started the engine, engaged gear and the pick-up moved forward. Muna and Waitherero waved and Janet waved back. After reaching the road, Waichari accelerated the pick-up. It hummed down the hill at a moderate speed. A cool wind hissed in through the half-open windows, and the sun climbed behind the clouds in the east, creating a golden glow.

Waichari looked ahead at the road, but he watched the girl through the corner of his eyes. She was also looking ahead, with her hands on her lap, but now and then she stole sidelong glances at him. Though she appeared at ease, he could feel she was tense.

'Nice day for a drive, don't you think?' Waichari asked.

'I do.'

'But it will get a little hot for comfort at midday.'

'Yes.'

Waichari gave up making polite conversation and lapsed into silence. Presently they reached Kangema trading centre and Waichari pulled up at the small petrol station. While the truck was being filled with petrol, he went to a nearby shop and bought copies of that day's editions of the *Daily Nation* and *The Standard*. He nodded with grim satisfaction at the headlines and their accompanying stories. Wekesa had done his work well after he had left him in Nairobi, but would the stories serve their purpose? They would have to wait and see.

Waichari folded the newspapers, went back to the pick-up and paid the service-man. The journey resumed, and so did the silence. After a few kilometres, Waichari found the silence intolerable. After all, he had offered to drive Waruguru to the provincial town to get an opportunity to converse with her. He decided to try again.

'So you are determined to go?'

'Yes, I am.'

'I am beginning to wonder if your eagerness to go away has not been urged by your hatred of me?'

'Hatred?' she asked in a pained voice. It was good to see expression in her face again. Even scorn was better than the indifference she had been showing him. 'I don't hate you. As a girl, the only inheritance I am to get from my father is education, and I am going to have it.'

'I see. How long will it take?'

'Two years. Look at those gardens. The crops have withered. The poor owners will not harvest anything this season.'

She was deliberately steering the conversation from herself and Waichari stopped questioning her for the time being. But after they had passed Sagana and Karatina, he realised they were going to reach their destination without his finding out what he wanted to know most from her. Choosing a lonely spot with bushes, he slowed down, moved off the road, stopped the vehicle and cut the engine.

'What's wrong?' she asked.

'The engine is too hot,' he lied. 'We have to let it cool down. Let us stretch our legs while it does.'

'Are you sure? The thing is still as good as new. Perhaps it needs water!'

'I want to talk to you in a better atmosphere,' he admitted.

'But I'll be late for college.'

'The college will have you for two years, Waruguru. Surely you can spare me five minutes.'

Reluctantly she got out of the vehicle and followed him as he strolled into the bushes in his slow manner. Presently he sat down and patted the ground beside him inviting her to do the same. Shyly, she obeyed. Birds chirped in the shrubs around while ahead stretched the majestic snow-capped Mount Kenya, looking blue in the cloudless morning sky.

'Before we part, there is a matter I want you to make clear,' he began, 'for it has troubled my mind greatly. So please let us be frank with one another. You know I've always liked you since you were a little girl, and we have always got on well together. Then your attitude towards me changed. You made a remark about my not being able to take care of someone else since I could not take care of my own affairs. I know I got into debt and disgrace, but I'd have expected you to be more understanding of how I had erred, for to err is to be human. Even now you've not forgiven me. Waitherero has. She hinted to me that there is something I've done you find hard to forgive. So the big question is, how can I have wronged you? Tell me the truth.'

While he had been talking, she had started fidgeting and breaking blades of grass.

'Very well.' She raised her expressive face to his lean one. 'You accuse me of despising you, but that's not really true. I've merely been angry with you. I've not been angry because you wronged me, but because you wronged yourself.'

'Wha–a–t?' he exclaimed in surprise. He had not expected such an answer.

She regarded him seriously for a while. 'I'll tell you how, since you insist we should be frank. You say you've liked me since I was a little girl. Well, I liked you even if you had your little failures. The love your family showed me made me feel like one of you. My parents watched me and didn't mind my coming to your place whenever I liked. I believe that they, like your father,were hoping we would make a match of it. When the auction was announced, everything was changed. My people began to sneer at you, but I ignored them. But when my parents turned against you too, I was upset.' She looked down. 'They forbade me ever to return to your place. That's why I was furious with you, and found it difficult to forgive you. I still find it so. You spoiled your name before my parents, and so destroyed our relationship.'

She looked up and saw how distressed he was. 'In spite of being forbidden to come to your place, I did come a few times, yet you keep accusing me of hatred. Are you being fair? And as for my remark about you not being able to take care of someone else, it was unfortunate and it was spurred by the anger of the moment. I was bitter because you disappointed my parents and so wrecked our chances. When you accuse me of misunderstanding you, aren't you being unfair again? Didn't I ask you to explain how you had got into the mess? I wanted to know and to understand, but you didn't explain anything, and it made me more furious than ever. I didn't want to see you again. I admit I decided to go to the college to run away from you. But I had to wait until yesterday and learn about your fate. I couldn't come to your place every day while you were away, since I had been forbidden to do so, but I had to come yesterday. Poor Waitherero couldn't understand why I had forsaken her. When I found you had saved your home in some way I was glad. I could go away with an easier mind. But since the harm is already done, I am still angry with you. Now perhaps you understand why I have been behaving the way I have.'

'Can't the harm be undone?' he asked her. 'Tell me what to do, for I don't want to lose you.'

'I think the best thing for you to do is work hard and get back into my father's good books. Show him by your actions that you can be as capable as your father was.'

'If I do this, will you consent to marry me?'

She didn't hesitate. 'Yes.'

The simple word filled him with joy such as he had never known. 'In the meantime, must you go on this course?'

'Yes. Just think about it. Since you're so business-minded, the course will be to our advantage. I could assist you in your work.'

He considered her suggestion and found it good. 'You're right. It's a deal, pretty girl. Let's seal it.' Before she knew what he was about, he held her by

139

the shoulders and kissed her on the lips in the best movie tradition.

'I love you very much, you know,' he muttered. A thought occurred to him and he released her. 'What have I done and said?' he asked, at himself. 'You have turned me into a sentimental softie of the worst kind!'

Since she was out of breath, Janet did not reply. she just smiled shyly at him.

'But I guess being a softie has its consolations,' he said, gathering her into his arms again.


In a wooden bungalow in a village in northern Uganda, Sowedi lay on his back in bed, cursing the Kenyan smugglers under his breath. They were the cause of his misfortune.

After they had released him near Chepkube, he had crossed back into Uganda on foot, and gone to his abandoned Mercedes. Furiously, he had driven back to Kampala and his residence. He had found his concubine and workers still tied and locked up, and he had released them. Then he had rung his office, and had learned what he had dreaded: Major Mulindwa had released Njogu and his crew. The major had been furious to learn he had been tricked into releasing his prisoners.

Sowedi had considered his position. Njogu was no simple man. The political repercussions Sowedi had feared would occur when Njogu's friends learned he had been tortured and robbed of his property. Worse, the Big Man was not going to be pleased to learn the prisoners had been released to go and make a noise at a time when Kenyan-Ugandan relations were hanging in the balance. The Big Man was not going to understand why they had been released (he was certainly not going to be told the truth). A plausible explanation had to be given, or he would suspect corruption. Talking of corruption, the Big Man would be even more displeased to learn where Njogu's seized property had gone. Njogu was sure to claim it when he recovered — if he recovered!

Knowing the Big Man, Sowedi had decided that the wisest course for him to take was to hide for a week and see the reaction from Kenya. If the worst happened, he would go to live in the Sudan or Zaire. Instructing his servants to report by phone if anyone came looking for him, Sowedi had gone to his place of business and his bank and collected all the money he could lay his hands on. Then he had driven with the woman to this remote village. No one except the servant and the woman knew he owned the bungalow.

Sowedi got out of bed, washed his face and combed his thinning hair. Then he dressed his slight figure carefully before going to the sitting room. The woman brought his breakfast tray, bowed as she set it before him in the traditional way, and sat on the floor while he ate. When he had finished, she rose to fetch a drink for him but, as she turned, the door burst open. She shrieked as half a dozen grim, pitch-black men in Kaunda suits stormed in. Two of them were brandishing pistols.

Sowedi stared in fascinated horror with a napkin suspended half-way to his mouth. He recognised the men and knew whom they served.

'Good morning, Colonel Sowedi,' said their leader. 'We thought we'd find you here. The Big Man wants to see you. He's in quite a hurry.'

Sowedi tried to speak but only managed an unintelligible noise. He felt a sickly feeling in his stomach while a shiver ran along his spine. This was the end. How had they found him so quickly? How stupid of him not have kept a look out! Like someone in a nightmare he felt his wrists handcuffed behind him.

As the hysterical girl was handcuffed also, Sowedi found his voice. 'No! Leave her alone. She has nothing to do with anything. She is just a street-walker I collected on my way here.'

'Silence, Colonel,' said the leader. 'She has a tongue, and she will speak for herself.' He gestured to four of his men. 'Search the house.'

After a swift but thorough search, the men came back with the suitcase full of money, a gun, some documents and little else. Then the prisoners were led out of the bungalow to a Land-Rover which had been parked outside the village.

Two and a half hours later their manacles were removed and they were led into a well-furnished hotel room. The Big Man was seated in the middle of the room, flanked by two top-ranking government officials in army uniforms. He was reading a newspaper. Behind him were a few more of the grim-faced men in suits. Sowedi looked at the bristling expession on the Big Man's face and his heart sank. But he had had time to gather his courage and he faced the Big Man calmly.

The Big Man put down the newspaper he had been reading and regarded Sowedi coldly. 'Ah, it is you at last, Colonel Sowedi. Where have you been?'

'At my holiday resort, Your Excellency. I have a

weak heart and my doctor recommended a few days' peace and quiet in the countryside.'

'You have a bigger threat to your health,' the Big Man said, and grinned grimly at the officers with him. He picked up the newspaper from the table and tossed it at Sowedi. 'Read the headlines and the editorial. I want an explanation.'

Sowedi froze and stared in dismay. It was that day's edition of the Kenyan newspaper, *Daily Nation*. The banner headline seemed to scream at him; KENYAN BUSINESSMAN TORTURED TO DEATH. There was a photograph of Njogu underneath, together with the story. It was all about the torment the Kenyans had undergone in the State Research Bureau. This kind of story was not unusual; what really frightened Sowedi was where Wekesa was quoted by the newspaper as alleging that stock worth a million shillings and vehicles worth over three million had been seized and kept by a Colonel Sowedi and a Major Mulindwa for personal purposes. With trembling hands Sowedi turned to the editorial. It bitterly reminded the world of the innocent people butchered under the jungle 'justice' of the dictatorial Ugandan regime and also asked how long people were going to stand by and watch the evil.

Despite his panic, Sowedi's sharp brain worked swiftly, then he threw the newspaper away, feigning anger. 'It is lies, all lies! What an ungrateful lot they are! I had them released on humanitarian grounds, and they know it. I intended to return their property, but now I won't, Your Excellency! Let it be confiscated by our government for damages! And to think I released them to avoid tarnishing Uganda's good name! I wish I had had their necks twisted!'

'What an admirable actor you are, Sowedi!' said the Big Man, grinning grimly again. 'You have almost convinced me, even if I know you're lying. You see, Major Mulindwa has confessed everything,' the Big Man boomed, banging the table and rising to his feet, his bulk quivering and his wrath terrible to behold. 'You and Major Mulindwa have let your country down at a time when we should be more careful, and you tried to enrich yourselves by corrupt methods. You will be burned alive with gasoline, since your carcasses would give colic to crocodiles. Take him away.'

He turned to the whimpering girl. 'What has she done?'

'She has helped Sowedi to spend the corruption money.'

'Then she must die, too.'

'No, no!' she shrieked. 'I've done nothing wrong! Please leave me alone!'

The Big Man dismissed her with a wave of his hand, and she was dragged away also. He waited until her screams faded away, then he turned to his officers.

'After this, I want corruption to be watched more carefully at the high level. Prisoners must not be allowed to escape to smear our good name. And remember, when you eliminate Kenyans or such enemies of the State, you must be discreet. Summon the pressmen.'

When the pressmen came, the Big Man told them, 'I wish to declare the allegations in today's Kenyan newspapers are nothing but malicious propaganda. They are made by enemies of Uganda who are envious of the peace, tranquility and prosperity prevailing in Uganda, and are bent on disrupting it. Mr Njogu was not killed in Uganda. We loved him, and we are profoundly shocked by his demise. We send our condolences. We love all East Africans. Are we not all brothers and sisters? Why should we kill our brothers and sisters? Uganda is bent on promoting good neighbourliness between our three sister states. All are welcome to come and visit our beautiful country and trade with us, in an atmosphere of love and security.'

A year later, in 1978, Daniel arap Moi became the President of Kenya. One of the first things he did on taking office was to order a crackdown on smuggling and corruption. Measures such as the sacking of the elements who allowed the rackets to go unchecked, and the banning of travel by night of heavy vehicles, were taken. Thus, the era of large scale smuggling came to an end.

There was another factor involved. The end of 1978 saw the end of the coffee boom which had been enjoyed since 1976. So the smugglers of Chepkube and such places had to close their markets and return to their respective occupations and countries. They bitterly resented this because they became poor, but school children praised the end of their notorious trade in song.

But smuggling is a disease which is impossible to cure, so a little went on over the years. The economic problems which continued in Uganda, even after the ousting of Idi Amin, did not help matters.

The healthy economic conditions of 1978, and

hard work, helped Waichari to clear his debts and put him on his feet. In the following year the conditions were not so good but, without the burden of debts, he was able to start progressing by increasing the stock of his store and resuming the construction of the house his father had started.

Gradually, people began to respect him as they had respected his father. Amongst them was Janet's father, who was the one who mattered most. When she finished her course, the old man did not object when she began to work for Waichari.

The third year was even worse, but Waichari put in more effort and he was able to keep on stocking his store and building his house, even if progress was slow.

Wekesa was running his affairs well and he and Waichari were still in contact. Chepkube had receded to the back to their minds. But now, three years after he had been there, Waichari recalled it as if he had seen it yesterday. With business being slack, he and Janet were in the back room of his store. He was reading a newspaper at the table and she was making coffee.

The newspaper carried a series of articles summarising the accomplishments of the *Nyayo* government. There was one item which held Waichari's interest. He looked at it for a long time and then laughed softly. Janet went over to him, stood behind him and studied the item which held his interest. It was a photograph of a few men surrounding an open sack of coffee. Beneath it was the caption *Heyday of Chepkube.*

'What's so funny about it?' Janet asked. 'I do not understand.'

146

'The photograph represents an era of smuggling which the *Nyayo* government terminated,' he explained.

'Why does it affect you so? Did you like *magendo*?'

'No, my dear, I didn't,' Waichari replied with truth. Though it had made him a lot of money when he was in trouble, he had no cause to miss *magendo* when it had been curbed.

'I still don't understand why the picture should hold so much interest for you,' said Janet.

'Forget it, it is not important.'

Janet returned to her pot, vexed. Waichari watched her, feeling guilty. He was not going to shock her now by telling the truth. Some day, after they were married and had got used to one another, he would confess to her that he had been one of the smugglers of Chepkube!

**PACESETTERS**

## The Border Runners

Waichari's parents are tragically killed in a car crash leaving him with huge debts and a younger brother and sister to care for. Their farm will have to be auctioned unless Waichari can find the money. There is only one way to get it quickly – Waichari will have to risk everything by joining the smuggling trade (*magendo*) at Chepkube on the Kenyan/Ugandan border. It is a dangerous game and he cannot even tell Janet, the girl he loves, what he is doing.

*The Authors*
*James Irungu and James Shimanyula*

James Irungu has written numerous plays for TV and short stories. He has won two competitions for writers organised by *Drum Magazine*.
James Shimanyula is a graduate of the London School of Journalism. As well as being a journalist he is also an historian and has worked as a teacher. He has written a number of articles which have been published in the *Sun*, the *Yorkshire Post*, the *Times of Zambia*, the *Herald* (Zimbabwe) and the *New Zealand Times*. He is Managing Editor of the Featureline Africa Press Agency in Nairobi.

Irungu and Shimanyula have been close friends for more than eight years. Their first play, *The Black Prophet*, has just been published. They are jointly working on two other plays.

**MACMILLAN**

ISBN 0-333-35412-5

90101>

9 780333 354124